TO: Dearest Lindsay

Our d... is a blessing ... God for y...

We hope that you will find this book to be both practical and low stress!

Love,
Mom & Dad Abc

Christmas 2016

Too
Blessed
to be
Stressed
Cookbook

Too Blessed to be Stressed
Cookbook

A Busy Woman's Guide to Stress-Free Cooking
(Prep Time 20 Minutes or Less!)

From Popular Inspirational Humorist
Debora M. Coty

BARBOUR BOOKS
An Imprint of Barbour Publishing, Inc.

Printed in association with the literary agency of WordServe Literary Group, Ltd., www.wordserveliterary.com

Published by Barbour Books, an imprint of Barbour Publishing, Inc., P.O. Box 719, Uhrichsville, Ohio 44683, www.barbourbooks.com

Our mission is to publish and distribute inspirational products offering exceptional value and biblical encouragement to the masses.

 Member of the Evangelical Christian Publishers Association

Printed in China.

"Prepare me the kind
of tasty food I like and
bring it to me to eat,
so that I may give
you my blessing."

GENESIS 27:4 NIV

Debora M. Coty

More Beauty Less Beast

Too Blessed to be Stressed

Fear, Faith, and a Fistful of Chocolate

Wit and Wisdom for Sidestepping Life's Worries

Too Loved to be Lost

Need a little help alleviating stress in other areas of your life besides the kitchen? Be sure to get copies of Deb's award-winning inspirational books, each available in print or e-version and chock-full of her unique brand of truth gift wrapped in humor:

Too Blessed to Be Stressed

More Beauty, Less Beast

Fear, Faith, and a Fistful of Chocolate

Too Loved to Be Lost

Acknowledgments

Sweetened condensed gratitude to the following friends and family who contributed recipes, which have created happy memories and become beloved traditions in our home: Adele Mitchell (a.k.a. Mama), Cricket and Josh Boyer, Rebecca Coty, Jane Ann Coty, Suzi Coty Beatty, Pat Glickman, Gloria Foster, Sandi Heath, Pam Cunningham, Cheryl Johnston, Julia Thomas, Jan McRae, Dianne Mullins and her sweet mom, Lila Rae Yawn, Sandi Dorey, Betty Combee, Marlene Costa, Charmaine Andrews, Cheryl Barber, and Jenna Barber, my health food guru friend who has more healthy recipes to share at www.skinnygirlcaneat.com.

Warm toasties to Trish Miller of Affairs of the Heart in Waynesville, North Carolina, and Randy Jordan of The Tole Booth who loaned me their delightful Kitchen Kwips.

Undiluted thanks to my writer buds who contributed quotes, recipes, and/or stories:

- ♥ Martha Bolton, author of 88 books (including *Cooking with Hot Flashes*) and Emmy-nominated writer for Bob Hope (15 years); www.MarthaBolton.com
- ♥ Cheri Cowell, author, speaker, and Sidewalk Theologian; www.CheriCowell.com
- ♥ Sharron Cosby, speaker and author of *Praying for Your Addicted Loved One*: *90 in 90*; www.efamilyrecovery.com
- ♥ Elizabeth Hoagland, creator of one of my favorite blogs, *Worship with Words*, which can be found at her website www.ElizabethHoagland.com
- ♥ Julie Morris, RN, author of *Guided by Him to a Thinner, Not So Stressed-Out You!*; www.GuidedbyHim.com

A heaping cup of hugs to my seasoned agent, Greg Johnson of WordServe Literary Agency, and to my hot and bubbly editor, Kelly McIntosh, at Barbour Publishing.

Lovin' spoonfuls to my long-suffering, uncomplaining husband, Chuck, who has consumed my culinary flops and victories with equal gusto for the past thirty-seven years.

✳ Hey, BFF

(Blessed Friend Forever),

I'd love to connect with you via Facebook, Twitter, my website, www.DeboraCoty.com, or my personal blog, *Living Life in the Crazy Lane,* www.DeboraCoty.blogspot.com.

Got any good recipes we can swap?

Introduction

Welcome to my girl cave (some call it a kitchen). I'm so glad you're here!

Like you, I've spent many years juggling my crazy-busy schedule, trying to take care of my family—and myself—by providing nutritional, creative, fun food that's so delicious my kids will want to serve it to their children one day. Of course, I made my share of mistakes (a few of my misadventures are included for your chuckling pleasure), but that's how we learn, right? This book is the fruit of four decades of labor.

Whether you're into health food or comfort food or something in-between, there are exciting recipes for you here in the four sections: Time-Wise, Soul-Fed, Heart-Healthy, and Company-Happy.

About fifteen years ago, Spouse decided to go vegetarian, so I've collected some super meatless recipes as well as the yummy, down-home pork, beef, fish, and chicken dishes passed along by my Southern mama and granny. Not to mention the tried-and-true nutritious quickie fare I've developed myself over the years to fit my crammed schedule.

But a girl's gotta have fun, right? Just wait till you get to the choc-tastic recipes!

So dig in. Within these pages you'll find lots of terrific simple, time-saving recipes, menu suggestions, and even grocery lists to help decom-stress your life. Each recipe requires only 20 minutes or less prep time, so you no longer have to be glued to your kitchen. Hey, it's time to stop treading water in the stress-pool of life and actually *enjoy* cooking. May your culinary blessings outweigh your stressings!

"This is my invariable advice to people:
learn how to cook—try new recipes,
learn from your mistakes,
be fearless, and above all have fun!"
JULIA CHILD

Basics for Stress-Free Cooking

Okay, dear stressed-out friend, let's get started. For the recipes in this cookbook, I'm jotting a list of the staples I'm going to assume you already have on hand. That means these staples won't be included in the grocery lists for the suggested menus (see pages 155–187) unless required in an unusual quantity or by a specific brand name.

By the way, do check out the recommended menus in the back of the book—a marvelous little feature to help you plan great meals a week at a time while saving time, energy, and needless *stress*.

Are you ready for some tummy-growling, saliva-flinging culinary adventures? In the immortal words of a certain curly haired kitchen heroine, *Bon appétit!*

Equipment*
(besides a working stove, of course)

electric mixer
food processor

microwave
slow cooker

(*Recommended but not absolutely necessary to create the culinary delights in this book.)

Terminology Used in This Book

Butter = butter or margarine unless specified "real butter"
Greased = coated with butter, oil, or cooking spray (in almost all recipes, I prefer spray)

Staples to Keep in Stock

allspice	nutmeg	chicken broth
cooking spray (like Pam)	salt & pepper	garlic (minced)
light brown sugar	baking powder	paprika
powdered sugar	eggs	teriyaki sauce
apple cider vinegar	onions	chili powder
cornstarch	seasoned salt	garlic powder
mayonnaise	baking soda	Parmesan cheese (grated)
rice (brown or white)	extra virgin olive oil	vanilla
bacon bits	onion flakes	cinnamon (ground)
cumin	soy sauce	Italian seasoning
milk	canola oil	parsley flakes
Ritz crackers	flour	Worcestershire sauce
baking cocoa	oregano	
dill weed	sugar	

These additional staples can be stored in your freezer so they're always available:

shredded cheddar cheese
whipped topping (tubs)
shelled pecans or walnuts

butter (best to keep one box of "real" salted butter sticks and one of cheaper margarine)

Section 1

Time-Wise

"Hunger is the best sauce in the world."
CERVANTES

"You will have plenty to eat,
until you are full,
and you will praise
the name of the
LORD your God."

JOEL 2:26 NIV

Dump Dishes

One-Stop Schlopping (Dinner in One Pan)

I was introduced to the concept of one-pan cooking when my first baby arrived. I visited a friend who, while we were chatting at her kitchen table and watching our babies crawl around on the floor, stood and walked over to her counter, dumped a few ingredients into a glass baking dish, popped it in the microwave, and within minutes placed before me a moist, luscious dessert with no muss, no fuss, and best of all, next to no cleanup.

Seemed like a dandy idea to me; not only would it save time, water, soap, and energy cleaning all those extra pots and mixing bowls, it would also free me up for more peek-a-boo time with my little one. How could this be a bad thing? (By the way, that very recipe—Magical Microwave Dessert—is included under "Good to Go" in the Time-Wise section).

So I became a dump cook. No, I didn't say *dumb* cook, although some may beg to differ. I began experimenting with dumping an entire meal together in one dish—meat, vegetables, starch, occasionally fruit, and oftentimes bread. Some of my efforts worked out famously and some. . .er, didn't. You might even call them infamous.

Like the night I came up with spinach-mango pizza. Sure seemed promising at the time. But I'm here to tell you that there are some flavors that flat refuse to join hands and tango. Nobody would eat the stuff. The kids retched. The dog took one sniff

and ran beneath the couch. I had to bury it in the backyard azalea bed. A week later I noticed my poor azaleas had withered like I'd watered them with lemon juice.

Okay, so you live and learn.

The one-pan idea is still a good one for promoting the three culinary *C*'s: combine, consolidate, and convenience. I hope you'll be motivated to experiment with your favorite food combinations and be sure to share them with me. (Unless, of course, your flower bed looks like it belongs to the Addams Family!)

*Disclaimer: Some of the following recipes may actually take *two* pans (one for prep and one for cooking), but I promise I'll keep the cleanup as minimal as possible.

The Easiest Way to Cook a Chicken

Since many of the recipes in this cookbook call for cooked chicken, I want to share this enormously helpful tip with you. The most stress-free way I've found to cook a chicken is to plop the whole bird (rinsed well and giblets removed) in your slow cooker with 1 cup water and a few dashes each of salt and pepper. So simple. Cook on low overnight while you're asleep and the meat not only falls off the bone the next morning, but you also have a nice broth to use for cooking pasta or rice. Freeze the meat in quart-size ziplock bags (about 2 cups each bag), and simply pull one out and defrost as needed. No muss, no fuss.

> *"Life expectancy would grow by leaps and bounds if green vegetables smelled as good as bacon."*
>
> DOUG LARSON

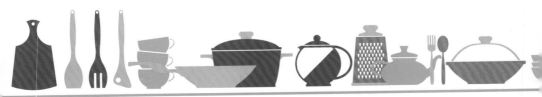

"Nobody Makes It Better" Pizza

PREP TIME: 10 minutes
COOKING TIME: 10 minutes in preheated 400° oven
SERVES: 4 to 6

1 (10½ ounce) can condensed tomato soup (I like Campbell's best)

1 premade pizza crust (my go-to brand is Mama Mary's Thin & Crispy pizza crusts, which come in a handy 2-pack)

8 ounces shredded cheddar cheese

8 ounces shredded mozzarella cheese

Grated Parmesan cheese

CHOOSE YOUR FAVE TOPPINGS:

Fresh or canned mushrooms (8 ounces, give or take to your preference)

9 ounces honey-roasted turkey breast or ham (lunch meat), chopped to postage stamp size

1 (20 ounce) can pineapple tidbits in pineapple juice

1 pound ground beef or turkey, browned and drained

4 ounces pepperoni (I use turkey pepperoni with 70 percent less fat than regular pepperoni)

Spread half of tomato soup (I use soup instead of tomato sauce for a milder, sweeter taste) on each crust; top with 2 to 3 of your chosen toppings. Top that with cheddar (you might consider reduced fat sharp cheddar if you're counting calories, although there's enough cheese on this thing to clog the English Channel) and mozzarella divided between the two pizzas. A generous sprinkling of Parmesan (use reduced fat if you want to save a few more calories to use on your sundae) on top is a sure winner. Bake for 10 minutes or until cheese melts. When you get a whiff of this happiness on a plate, you'll slobber all over yourself like one of Pavlov's dogs.

"God ordered the world and all things on it; I ordered a pizza and all things on it."
JAROD KINTZ

Quick as a Wink Stir-Fry

PREP TIME: 10 minutes
COOKING TIME: 15 minutes on stove top
SERVES: 4 to 6

✱ This tasty and healthy dish was my go-to dinner during the always-pinched-for-time years our kids were growing up. They called it Moo Goo in My Pan. I tweaked the original recipe many times to end up with this one, which was frequently requested (and still is whenever my kids come to visit). It's also an excellent source of vitamins A and C.

4 tablespoons soy sauce (about 10 shakes of the bottle)

2 tablespoons cornstarch

½ teaspoon sugar

½ teaspoon garlic powder

1 to 2 pounds raw boneless, skinless chicken breasts cut into bite-size chunks (I buy whole breasts or breast strips when they're on sale and freeze them)

4 tablespoons extra virgin olive oil, divided

6 to 8 ounces sliced fresh mushrooms (buy them already sliced)

1 medium onion, sliced into ⅛-inch strips

1 red bell pepper, sliced into strips (optional)

1 (12 ounce) bag frozen stir-fry veggies (usually includes broccoli florets, snow peas, julienned carrots, bean sprouts, or various other ready-to-cook veggies)

Teriyaki sauce (optional)

Handful cashews (optional)

2 cups cooked white rice (I use Minute rice; start cooking it first thing per package directions and it'll be finished and ready to devour when the meat and veggies are done)

In small mixing bowl, stir soy sauce, cornstarch, sugar, and garlic powder until slightly thickened (may need to add a little more cornstarch if it's really runny); then add chicken and set aside to marinate while you cook the veggies. If you have more meat than sauce, just add extra soy sauce until all meat is covered (don't worry—it's not an exact science; it'll turn out great).

In 12-inch skillet (or wok if you have one), heat 2 tablespoons olive oil over medium-high heat until it sizzles when you drop in a mushroom slice. Add veggies, stirring quickly and frequently until tender, not mushy (about 5 minutes). Pour veggies into large mixing bowl and set aside (okay, I'll admit there's more than one bowl in this recipe, but it can't be helped unless you want to marinate the chicken in the dog's dish and pour the hot veggies in your husband's lap).

In same skillet, add remaining 2 tablespoons olive oil, then marinated meat. Stir constantly (chicken will try to stick to pan) until meat turns whitish in color (cut a piece in half to make sure it's not raw inside). Return veggie mixture to skillet and cook with meat for 2 to 3 minutes. I like to add a few dollops of teriyaki sauce at this point for a little more Asian zing (but this is optional). Stir in cashews last, and serve over bed of rice.

"After all the trouble you go to, you get about as much actual 'food' out of eating an artichoke as you would from licking 30 or 40 postage stamps."
MISS PIGGY

Beef 'n' Bean Bonanza

✳Howdy, pardner! This one's for the hungry wranglers in your corral.

PREP TIME: 10 minutes
COOKING TIME: 10 minutes in microwave
SERVES: 4 to 6

1 pound lean ground beef

1 medium onion, chopped

2 (15 ounce) cans pork and beans (nothing fancy, just regular ole pork and beans); don't drain

8 ounces sliced fresh mushrooms

1 (10½ ounce) can condensed tomato soup

Brown beef and onion in large skillet; drain. Add beans, mushrooms, and soup; mix well. Pour into greased microwavable baking dish and cook covered at medium power level for 10 minutes. Best if consumed wearing cowboy boots and hat.

"Only a fool argues with a skunk, a mule, or a cook."
OLD COWBOY SAYING

Everybody's Fave Baked Spaghetti

PREP TIME: 15 minutes
COOKING TIME: 30 minutes in preheated 350° oven
SERVES: 6 to 8

1 (16 ounce) box spaghetti noodles (I like angel hair)

1 pound ground beef or turkey (I use turkey)

1 small onion, chopped

2 (10½ ounce) cans condensed tomato soup

1 (10½ ounce) can cream of mushroom soup

1 (4 ounce) can mushrooms (or fresh mushrooms are even better)

4 tablespoons Worcestershire sauce

3 cups shredded cheddar cheese

½ soup can water

½ cup grated Parmesan cheese

Boil noodles according to package directions. While they're cooking, brown meat and onion in large skillet; drain. Add soups, mushrooms, and Worcestershire sauce, mixing well. Sprinkle in cheddar cheese gradually, reserving 1 cup. Stir in water and simmer for 5 minutes, stirring occasionally. Add cooked noodles (rinsed and drained) to meat mixture and pour into greased 9x13-inch baking pan. Cover with foil and bake for 20 minutes. Remove foil and sprinkle with remaining cup of cheese and Parmesan and return to oven for 10 more minutes. For potlucks, double the recipe.

"Everything you see I owe to spaghetti."
SOPHIA LOREN

Impossible Meat Pie

PREP TIME: 10 minutes
COOKING TIME: 35 minutes in preheated 400° oven
SERVES: 6 to 8

✳ *When I fix this, I always think fondly of my friend Nancy who shared this delicious meal-in-one-pan recipe with me three decades ago.*

1 (10 ounce) package frozen chopped broccoli (may substitute frozen or canned mixed veggies)

½ cup chopped onion

1 cup shredded cheddar cheese

1 pound lean ground beef or turkey

1½ cups milk (low fat okay)

¾ cup baking mix (I like Bisquick)

1 teaspoon chopped parsley

3 large eggs

Salt and pepper to taste

Prepare broccoli per package directions; drain. Spoon into greased pie plate or baking dish along with onion and cheese; spread evenly. Beat remaining ingredients with mixer or blender until smooth (less than 1 minute). Pour into dish over veggies. Bake until golden brown, about 35 minutes; let stand 5 minutes before cutting.

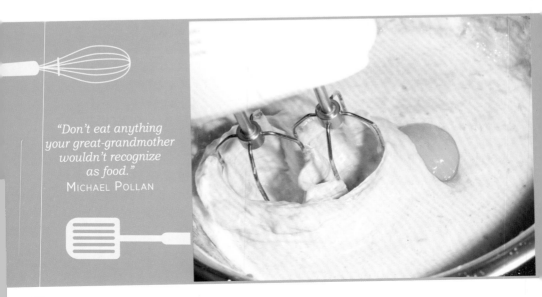

"Don't eat anything your great-grandmother wouldn't recognize as food."
MICHAEL POLLAN

Orzo-Veggie Chick-er-ole

PREP TIME: 15 minutes
COOKING TIME: 20 minutes in preheated 350° oven
SERVES: 4 (you can easily double recipe for 8)

1 cup uncooked orzo (pasta shaped like rice)

1 (12 ounce) steam-in-bag broccoli or mixed veggies

1 (10½ ounce) can cream of chicken soup

2 tablespoons mayonnaise (light okay)

½ cup milk (low fat okay)

1 cup chopped cooked chicken

Ritz crackers, crushed

Cook orzo per package instructions (takes about 10 minutes); drain. While orzo is cooking, microwave veggies according to package directions (about 6 minutes). In mixing bowl, combine soup, mayonnaise, and milk. Add cooked orzo and chicken, then veggies. Spoon into greased 1-quart baking dish and top with crackers. Bake for 20 minutes.

Chuckle Break:

Gender-Neutral Sandwiches, Anyone?

My hometown BFF Jan was watching her eight-year-old grandson, Mason, and his three-year-old sister, Gracie, one day when this interesting conversation took place:

Jan: So who's hungry? What would y'all like for lunch?

No answer from either kid.

Jan: Well, let's see. . . Mason, would you like a grilled-cheese sandwich?

Gracie, the drama queen: *No*, Mimi, he's a BOY. He gets a BOY-cheese sandwich. I'm a GURL. I get the GURL-cheese sandwich.

*A simple but all-inclusive meal that tastes great.

Workday Salvation

PREP TIME: 15 minutes
COOKING TIME: 20 minutes in preheated 350° oven
SERVES: 4 to 6

1 pound ground beef or turkey

1 medium onion, chopped

1 egg

2 cups cheddar cheese spread (shredded cheddar cheese works, too)

1 (10 ounce) package frozen chopped spinach, thawed and drained (may substitute broccoli)

2 cups cooked rice (white or brown; I use Minute rice)

½ teaspoon salt and pepper to taste (garlic and seasoned salt are lovely, too)

Brown meat with onion in skillet; drain well. Turn off heat and add egg and cheese by spoonfuls. Stir in other ingredients. Turn mixture into greased 1½-quart baking dish; bake covered for 20 minutes.

"We all eat, and it would be a sad waste of opportunity to eat badly."
ANNA THOMAS

29

Starke Raving Chicken

PREP TIME: 15 minutes
COOKING TIME: 30 minutes in preheated 350° oven
SERVES: 4 to 6

✱ This is one of my mama's standby chicken recipes, named after Starke, Florida, my beloved hometown. I added potatoes to round out the meal. Trust me, you'll love it!

1 pound raw chicken strips

8 ounces shredded Swiss cheese (or Swiss cheese slices)

1 (10½ ounce) can cream of chicken soup

½ cup chicken broth (or 3 chicken bouillon cubes mixed in ½ cup boiling water)

1 cup crushed Stove Top Stuffing (crush it while it's still in the bag)

⅓ cup butter, melted

6 to 8 small Honey Gold potatoes (or new red potatoes), rinsed and dried

Layer chicken strips in greased 9x13-inch pan. Layer Swiss cheese on top of chicken. Mix soup and broth together and pour over cheese. Top with crushed stuffing, then drizzle melted butter over stuffing. Place potatoes on microwave-safe platter; pierce each potato with a fork and microwave on high for 5 minutes. Tuck mostly cooked potatoes around outer edges of chicken, spooning a little sauce from bottom of pan over each. (Honey Gold potatoes by Tasteful Selections boasts "buttery sweet flavor with velvety golden flesh and delicate skin." They really are delicious.) Bake for 30 minutes.

*Household Hint:
If it walks out of your
kitchen, let it go.*

Since ready-made piecrusts come in a 2-pack, you can easily double this recipe to make 2 quiches; I use it regularly for guest brunches, lovely light lunches with my girlfriends, and easy evening family fare when I have as much energy as a squashed kumquat.

Incredibly Easy Quiche

PREP TIME: 10 minutes
COOKING TIME: 30 to 35 minutes in preheated 375° oven
SERVES: 4 (or 8 if doubled)

1 ready-made refrigerated piecrust (I prefer Pillsbury brand because it stores well in your freezer until someone surprises you with a visit and voilà! Just defrost, unroll a crust, and a tasty, elegant meal is on the way!)

3 eggs, beaten with a whisk (or 4 if you like it really rich)

2 cups milk (low fat okay, but more milk fat makes for a firmer, creamier quiche)

1 tablespoon dry onion flakes

1 teaspoon seasoned salt (and/or your favorite seasoning)

½ to 1 cup diced turkey, ham, or cooked bacon (quantity to your preference; squeeze extra water out of turkey or ham if lunch meat slices are used)

1 cup grated cheese of your choice (I use either sharp cheddar or 4-cheese Mexican blend for a little zing)

Note: You can make perfectly enjoyable meatless quiche by replacing the meat with finely chopped veggies and/or a variety of grated cheeses. Go ahead. . .be creative!

Unroll piecrust and lay in greased pie pan; trim edges to fit. In small mixing bowl, whisk eggs, milk, and spices together. Spread meat over crust in pie pan; sprinkle cheese over meat. Pour egg mixture over meat and cheese; make sure all ingredients are covered with egg mixture before popping into preheated oven. Bake for 30 to 35 minutes until center is firm and top begins to turn golden brown. Let cool at least 5 minutes (10 is better) before cutting (quiche will come out of the oven a bit poufy but will settle into a normal pie shape as it cools).

Wherein ye greatly rejoice, though now for a season, if need be, ye are in heaviness through manifold temptations.
1 PETER 1:6 KJV

Mexican Salad

❋*This post-busy-day recipe is super easy, kid friendly, and easily doubled for larger groups. Note the cooking time—only 7 minutes!*

PREP TIME: 10 minutes
COOKING TIME: 7 minutes on stove top
SERVES: 4 to 6

1 cup cooked rice (Minute rice is easiest)

1 small onion, diced

1 tablespoon olive oil or butter (or use Parkay vegetable oil spray instead for zero trans fat and cholesterol)

2 (15 ounce) cans Hormel chili without beans

1 (9 ounce) bag Fritos (you won't use the entire bag so feel free to munch while prepping)

½ head lettuce, shredded

1 large tomato, diced (or canned diced tomatoes are fine)

2 cups shredded 4-cheese Mexican blend

While rice is cooking, sauté onion in olive oil or butter in a 12-inch skillet until tender; add chili and stir, heating through. Layer Fritos, rice, meat mixture, lettuce, tomato, and, last, cheese in 2-quart serving bowl, and dive in. *Olé!*

"The discovery of a new dish does more for the happiness of the human race than the discovery of a star."
JEAN ANTHELME BRILLAT-SAVARIN

Kicky Quickie Pasta Salad

PREP TIME: 10 minutes
COOKING TIME: 10 minutes on stove top
SERVES: 6 to 8

1 (12 ounce) box rotini pasta

1 each red, yellow, and orange bell peppers, diced

1 (15 ounce) can black olives, pitted and halved

1 large bottle Italian dressing (your favorite flavor)

3 ounces artichoke hearts

8 ounces feta cheese, crumbled

8 ounces pepper jack cheese, shredded

2 to 3 ounces pepperoni (may use turkey or regular pepperoni)

Grape tomatoes (optional)

Prepare pasta per package directions; drain. Pour into large serving bowl. Add other ingredients, tossing lightly. And believe it or not, you're done!

This is terrific for covered dish dinners or picnics because you don't have to heat it.

Working Woman's Wall Plaque: Let's pretend! I'll pretend I like to cook. . .you pretend you like to eat it!

Crispy Cheddar Chicken

PREP TIME: 10 minutes
COOKING TIME: 35 minutes in preheated 400° oven
SERVES: 4 to 6

❋ My daughter Cricket's favorite family-feeding chicken recipe because there's hardly any prep time and the finished product is juicy and crunchy-licious.

4 raw boneless, skinless chicken breasts

½ cup milk (low fat okay)

½ cup shredded cheddar cheese

10 Ritz crackers, crushed

MAKE YOUR OWN SAUCE:

2 tablespoons butter

1 (10½ ounce) can cream of chicken soup

4 ounces sour cream (light okay)

—OR—

BUY SAUCE:

1 jar Ragu Parmesan Alfredo sauce (use Ragu Light Parmesan Alfredo if you're watching calories)

Dip and roll chicken breasts into three bowls in this order: milk, cheese, and crackers. Place cracker-coated chicken pieces in baking pan, cover with foil, and bake for 35 minutes until crispy. Five minutes before serving, combine sauce ingredients in a saucepan over medium-high heat until blended well (or open jar of Alfredo sauce). Pour over chicken just before serving, or serve in a pretty bowl on the side.

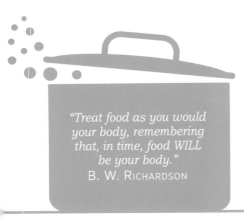

"Treat food as you would your body, remembering that, in time, food WILL be your body."
B. W. RICHARDSON

Fabulous 15-Minute Fettuccine

PREP TIME: 15 minutes
COOKING TIME: 10 minutes on stove top
SERVES: 4 to 6

1 (8 ounce) box fettuccine noodles

½ stick (4 tablespoons) butter

1 medium onion, sliced into thin strips

1 tablespoon Worcestershire sauce

1 pound peeled, deveined raw shrimp (can use frozen/thawed or fresh); or 4 raw boneless, skinless chicken breasts, cubed

1 (4 ounce) can sliced mushrooms, drained; or handful of sliced fresh mushrooms

1 tablespoon minced garlic (a fresh clove is great if you have one)

8 ounces sour cream (light okay)

½ teaspoon parsley flakes

½ cup grated Parmesan cheese, divided

Boil pasta according to package directions while you're cooking the shrimp (or chicken): Melt butter in large skillet at medium-high heat; add onions, Worcestershire sauce, and shrimp. Sauté for 5 minutes, then add mushrooms and garlic; cook for 5 more minutes or until meat is done.

In large serving bowl, combine cooked and drained pasta, sour cream, and parsley and mix until noodles are well coated. Stir in half of Parmesan cheese and shrimp or chicken and mix well. Sprinkle remainder of Parmesan on top and serve immediately. *Fabuloso!*

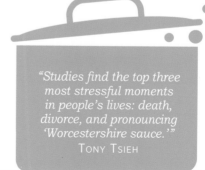

"Studies find the top three most stressful moments in people's lives: death, divorce, and pronouncing 'Worcestershire sauce.'"
TONY TSIEH

Deb's Delicious Teriyaki Pork

PREP TIME: 10 minutes
COOKING TIME: 6 to 8 hours in slow cooker on low
SERVES: a small army

½ to ¾ cup teriyaki sauce (I like Kikkoman)

1 pork roast, any size (I prefer a Boston butt but will buy whatever cut is on sale)

⅓ cup water

Minced garlic (I use the kind in a jar, but garlic powder works perfectly well)

Can you believe that's all?

＊*This you-can't-blow-it, ridiculously simple meat dish has been my go-to for years when I'm busy all day, company's coming, or I want to take a nice dinner to someone who's ill. Sorry if the directions aren't precise, but this one's not rocket science. Seriously, you cannot mess it up, and everybody will think you're the best cook ever. Tip: Buy a little bigger roast than you need so you'll have leftovers for delicious barbecue (next page).*

Cover bottom of slow cooker with teriyaki sauce. Pierce roast all around with a long-tined fork and then turn in sauce, coating each side. Pick a side to leave facing bottom of pot (if there's a fat-covered surface, I usually place it facing one side so the naked meat is able to soak up the sauce on the bottom of the pot). Add water to liquid in bottom, being careful not to wash sauce off meat. Add a few more shakes of teriyaki sauce to all sides of the meat you can reach. Coat top side of meat with thick layer of garlic. Cover with lid.

If I'm going to be around, I like to jump-start the cooking by setting the slow cooker on high for an hour then turning it down to low for the remainder of the day. If not possible, just leave on low the entire time. Serve in juice. The roast can cook up to 10 hours and still turn out beautifully. Your house will smell so heavenly when you come home, you'll expect to find Papa God sitting at your table with a fork in His hand and a grin on His face.

*Never again wonder
what to do with
leftover roast!*

Lip-Smacking Barbecue

Microwave meat for 2 minutes (assuming your leftover teriyaki pork roast was in the fridge) and drain off most of juice, leaving a smidge for moistness and flavor. With a sharp knife, chip roast into small, bite-size pieces (you can try a food processor, but the moist meat tends to gum mine up so I prefer a knife). Add equal parts of your fave brand barbecue sauce and ketchup to taste (lean more heavily on the sauce if you like a sharp bite to your barbecue; more ketchup if you prefer mild). There now. You're good to go!

"A woman is like a tea bag; you never know how strong she is until she gets in hot water."
NANCY REAGAN

Honey Mustard Chicken & Veggies

PREP TIME: 15 minutes
COOKING TIME: 4 hours on high or 8 hours on low in slow cooker
SERVES: 4 to 6

3 to 4 raw skinless chicken breasts

¼ cup brown sugar

3 large potatoes, washed and cut into bite-size chunks

3 carrots, sliced

½ cup honey (may substitute maple syrup if your larder is honeyless)

¼ cup honey mustard (may substitute Dijon mustard)

Salt and pepper to taste

1 cup shredded mozzarella cheese

Bacon bits

Coat slow cooker with cooking spray; place chicken in bottom. Sprinkle brown sugar on top of chicken (rub it in with your fingers) then veggies on top of that. In small bowl, mix honey, mustard, and salt and pepper; pour over veggies. Cook on high for 4 hours or on low for 8 hours. About 10 to 15 minutes before serving, sprinkle mozzarella cheese and bacon bits on top and continue cooking until cheese melts. Serve with extra honey mustard sauce from bottom of slow cooker.

"Cooking is like love. It should be entered into with abandon or not at all."
HARRIET VAN HORNE

Creamy Potatoes Au Gratin

PREP TIME: 15 minutes
COOKING TIME: 4 to 6 hours in slow cooker on low
SERVES: 4 to 6

2 tablespoons butter

1½ cups milk

2 tablespoons flour

5 to 6 potatoes, sliced

1 onion, diced

8 ounces shredded cheddar cheese

To make sauce: melt butter in small saucepan on medium-high heat; gradually stir in milk and flour, stirring constantly until thickened.

Coat slow cooker with cooking spray. Layer in this order: sliced potatoes, onions, cheese, sauce; repeat. Cook on low for 4 to 6 hours until potatoes are tender.

"How can you govern a country which has 246 varieties of cheese?"
CHARLES DE GOUILLE

French Dip

PREP TIME: 10 minutes
COOKING TIME: 8 hours in slow cooker on low
SERVES: 8

3 pounds beef roast

½ cup water

½ cup soy sauce

1 medium onion, halved

1 teaspoon minced garlic

1 teaspoon pepper

1 teaspoon dried thyme

1 teaspoon dried rosemary

8 slices provolone cheese

8 (4- to 6-inch) sub rolls

Pierce beef with long-tined fork; mix water and soy sauce together in bottom of slow cooker; add onion and sprinkle dry seasonings over roast. Cook until beef shreds with two forks, about 8 hours on low. Drain the sauce into au jus bowls. Layer beef and cheese on rolls and serve au jus (with dipping sauce from slow cooker).

"Everything that lives and moves about will be food for you. Just as I gave you the green plants, I now give you everything."
GENESIS 9:3 NIV

Chuckle Break:
Gettin' Chili in Here

Last yuletide, I came up with the idea of cooking a pot of homemade chili in the slow cooker while we were at church on Christmas Eve. I have a no-fail chili recipe and a slow cooker the size of a swimming pool—hey, what could go wrong?

With ten extended family members in tow, it seemed like a great idea; we could enjoy the worship service unhindered by hurry, worry, or stress, and then come home to the fragrant aroma of a delicious dinner all ready for the munching.

So I dressed for church early, and while everyone else was getting ready, I prepared the chili, making sure to double the batch and fill my jumbo-size slow cooker to the brim.

But something didn't look right. The soup looked too, well, soupy. Who likes runny chili? It's supposed to have rich, bountiful body. It should be thick enough to stick to your ribs and give your tongue a workout licking it off the spoon. Something must have gone awry when I doubled the recipe.

So in never-say-die mode, I added cornstarch to thicken the concoction. Seemed sensible, right? One heaping tablespoon. Two. Aw, heck—four for good measure. Then I plopped the lid back on and scurried out to the car cheerfully singing, "'Tis the season to be jolly. . ."

When we arrived back home, the house indeed smelled heavenly. In high spirits and with taste buds tingling (I'm pretty sure I saw dribbles of saliva exiting the corners of a mouth or two), everyone grabbed a bowl and eagerly lined up at the chili pot. Brandishing my festive red ladle, I removed the lid and reached in to scoop out the first sumptuous serving.

But what was this? My ladle bounced back off the surface of the chili like a basketball rimshot.

With five-alarm dismay, I discovered that my chili had congealed into a solid rubber block. Seriously, you could have jumped onto it from a three-story building and bounced back up to the roof.

This is how I learned about the super powers of cornstarch. A culinary lesson to remember about cooking chili: Thick = good. Goodyear = bad.

> *"Chili represents your three stages of matter:*
> *solid, liquid, and eventually gas."*
> Roseanne

My favorite chili recipe for fam or company (it's actually a melding of several recipes). You're gonna love this. . .zesty chili plus savory potatoes in every bite!

Humdinger Chili

PREP TIME: 15 minutes
COOKING TIME: 4 hours in slow cooker on low
SERVES: 6 to 8

2 pounds lean ground beef or turkey (I use turkey)

1 medium onion, chopped

1 green bell pepper, chopped (optional)

1 (14½ ounce) can diced tomatoes (may use combo diced tomato/peppers if desired)

2 (10½ ounce) cans tomato soup

1 (15 ounce) can Ranch Style beans

1 (15 ounce) can kidney beans (light or dark red)

1 package chili seasoning (mild, medium, or hot) or 3 tablespoons chili powder

1½ cups water

1 large potato, peeled and coarsely diced

Sour cream and grated cheddar cheese for garnishing

Brown beef or turkey with onion; drain. Combine with all other ingredients in slow cooker and cook for 4 hours on low until potatoes are soft. Serve garnished with sour cream and cheese. And as I learned in the preceding disaster story, whatever you do, DON'T ADD CORNSTARCH.

"If this is coffee, please bring me tea; but if this is tea, please bring me coffee."
ABRAHAM LINCOLN

Cricket's Breakfast Casserole

PREP TIME: 15 minutes
COOKING TIME: 4 hours in slow cooker on high
SERVES: 12

✳ My daughter, Cricket, came up with this recipe, too. We love it for dinner as much as breakfast, and it makes a ton!

1 (26 to 32 ounce) package frozen shredded hash brown potatoes

2 pounds ground sausage (our fave is Jimmy Dean), browned and drained

2 cups shredded mozzarella cheese

2 cups shredded cheddar cheese

½ cup grated Parmesan cheese

12 large eggs

½ cup milk (low fat okay)

½ teaspoon salt

¼ teaspoon pepper

½ cup bacon bits

Coat 6-quart (or larger) slow cooker with cooking spray. Layer half of potatoes on bottom; top with half of browned sausage, mozzarella, cheddar, and Parmesan cheeses.

Whisk together eggs, milk, salt, and pepper in large bowl and pour half over potato-sausage mixture. Repeat layers: potatoes, sausage, eggs. Sprinkle bacon bits on top before covering with lid. Cook for 4 hours on high or until eggs are set. Wonderful served with fruit and muffins.

"You don't have to cook fancy or complicated masterpieces—just good food from fresh ingredients."
JULIA CHILD

*Another outstanding dish we look forward to at Cricket's house.

Parmesan Chicken and Pasta

PREP TIME: 10 minutes
COOKING TIME: 8 to 10 hours on low or 4 to 5 hours on high in slow cooker
SERVES: 4 to 6

1 cup Italian seasoned bread crumbs

¼ cup Parmesan cheese

6 to 8 raw boneless, skinless chicken breasts, cut into 2-inch strips

1 (24 ounce) jar spaghetti or marinara sauce (your favorite brand)

1 cup shredded mozzarella cheese

8 ounces penne pasta (or your favorite style pasta)

Combine bread crumbs and Parmesan cheese in medium bowl; rinse chicken pieces with water, then dredge chicken through crumbs until well coated. Place in bottom of greased slow cooker. Pour spaghetti sauce over chicken; if chicken is in layers, pour a little sauce between each layer. Cook 8 to 10 hours on low or 4 to 5 hours on high. About 10 minutes before serving, sprinkle mozzarella cheese over chicken and replace lid. Cook pasta per package directions. When pasta is done, cheese should be melted and chicken will be ready to devour.

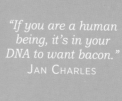

"If you are a human being, it's in your DNA to want bacon."
JAN CHARLES

Pizza in a Pot

*All the tasty ingredients of a pizza in one carefree slow cooker pot.

PREP TIME: 10 minutes
COOKING TIME: 4 hours in slow cooker on low
SERVES: 4 to 6

1 (24 ounce) jar spaghetti or marinara sauce (your favorite brand)

1 cup water

1 egg

2 tablespoons parsley

2 cups shredded mozzarella cheese, divided

¼ cup grated Parmesan cheese, divided

15 ounces ricotta cheese (low fat okay)

1 (4 ounce) can mushrooms (optional)

1 (7 ounce) packet dry Italian dressing

4 ounces Italian-style pepperoni slices (may use chicken pepperoni)

6 regular lasagna noodles, uncooked

Using electric mixer on low, combine sauce, water, egg, parsley, ½ cup mozzarella, 2 tablespoons Parmesan, ricotta, mushrooms, and dry dressing in large mixing bowl. When mixture is smooth, fold in pepperoni using a spoon (not mixer) so that pepperoni stays whole.

Coat slow cooker with cooking spray; pour in half the meat mixture. Top with 3 uncooked lasagna noodles, broken to fit, and ½ cup mozzarella cheese. Repeat another layer: remainder of meat mixture, 3 noodles broken to fit, 1 cup mozzarella, and remainder of Parmesan. Cover with lid and simmer on low for 4 hours or until noodles are soft.

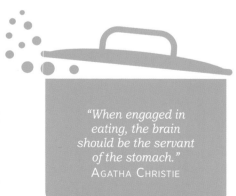

"When engaged in eating, the brain should be the servant of the stomach."
AGATHA CHRISTIE

✳ *When I served this super simple, slightly spicy soup to my eighty-eight-year-old daddy, his after-dinner comment was, "Every time I burp, my tonsils feel like they're catching fire." (Don't worry—unless you add Tabasco sauce, it's really not hot!)*

Taco Soup

PREP TIME: 10 minutes
COOKING TIME: 4 to 6 hours in slow cooker on low
SERVES: 6 to 8

1 (10½ ounce) can cream of chicken soup

1 (10 ounce) can mild green enchilada sauce

1 cup chicken broth

1 packet mild taco seasoning

Dash or two of Tabasco sauce (optional—if you like a kick)

Tortilla strips (can usually find in the salad toppings aisle)

Sour cream (light is okay)

1 (15½ ounce) can black beans, drained

1 (15½ ounce) can pinto beans, drained

1 (14½ ounce) can petite diced tomatoes, drained

1 (15 ounce) can whole kernel corn, drained

1 (12 ounce) can chunk chicken breast (break chunks into flakes with fork)

Combine all but tortilla strips and sour cream in slow cooker and stir until blended. Cook 4 to 6 hours on low. Ladle into bowls and top with dollop of sour cream and sprinkling of tortilla strips. To keep it simple, serve with salad, sliced fruit, and cheesy garlic bread. And a fire extinguisher for elderly relatives.

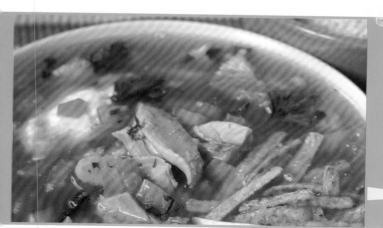

"Red meat is NOT bad for you. Now blue-green meat, THAT'S bad for you!"
TOMMY SMOTHERS

Incredibly Easy Cheesecake

PREP TIME: 10 minutes
COOKING TIME: none, refrigerate
SERVES: 16 (8 per pie)

16 ounces cream cheese (light okay)

½ cup sugar

12 ounces whipped topping (light okay)

2 ready-made graham cracker crusts (chocolate cookie piecrusts are excellent, too)

1 (21 ounce) can cherry or strawberry pie filling (light okay)

With electric mixer on medium-low, mix cream cheese, sugar, and whipped topping until smooth. Pour half into each piecrust. Top with pie filling (1 can will divide among 2 pies or you may use 2 cans if you like your topping extra thick); refrigerate until ready to serve.

Whoa. Can you believe that's all there is to it? I guarantee your family and guests won't believe it either as they gobble it up.

Our mouths were filled with laughter,
our tongues with songs of joy.
PSALM 126:2 NIV

Magical Microwave Dessert

PREP TIME: 5 minutes
COOKING TIME: 15 minutes in microwave
SERVES: 6

2 cans pie filling, any one flavor (I recommend apple, cherry, or strawberry)

1 cake mix, any flavor

1 stick (8 tablespoons) butter, melted

In greased 2½-quart casserole dish, layer 1 can pie filling on bottom, then ½ dry cake mix. Repeat. Pour butter over top and cook on high in microwave for 15 minutes or until cake appears done and dessert is bubbly. Decadent when served with a scoop of vanilla ice cream on top.

"The only time to eat diet food is while you're waiting for the steak to cook."
JULIA CHILD

Chocolate Blobs

PREP TIME: 5 minutes
COOKING TIME: 5 minutes on stove top
SERVES: 10 to 12

＊My kids affectionately dubbed these uber easy treats Chocolate Blobs on long-ago Sunday afternoons when we made them together.
Tip: Don't cut corners on the ingredients or they might not harden. But if they don't, just enjoy them with a spoon!

1 stick (8 tablespoons) butter

2 cups sugar

½ cup milk (low fat okay)

3 tablespoons baking cocoa

2½ cups oats

1 cup smooth peanut butter (optional)

¼ cup coconut (optional)

Melt butter in saucepan over medium-high heat; stir in sugar, milk, and cocoa. Bring to a hard boil; boil 1½ minutes. Remove from burner and add oats and, if desired, peanut butter and/or coconut (my little ones didn't like coconut so we omitted it, and the blobs turned out just as yummy). Mix well and immediately spoon walnut-size blobs onto wax paper (run a damp sponge over counter first and wax paper will stay in place). Blobs set in about 15 minutes; may refrigerate to speed up hardening process.

Chuckle Break:
Chocolate Repairs Relationship Cracks

*"When an argument breaks out with your spouse or BFF,
haul out your fave chocolate bar and share it. By the time
you're finished, nerves are calmer, voices are lower,
and you're both in a much more agreeable mood."*
DEBORA M. COTY, FROM *TOO LOVED TO BE LOST*

Cheese Crispies

PREP TIME: 5 minutes
COOKING TIME: 10 minutes in preheated
  350° oven
SERVES: 8 to 10

2 sticks (1 cup) butter

2 cups flour

2 cups Rice Krispies cereal

2 cups shredded sharp cheddar cheese

✴ *These breezy-cheesy nonsweet cookies were always Aunt Lala's annual contribution to the family Christmas gathering. Incredibly simple with their 2-2-2-2 ingredient measurements, I find them rather addictive. . .a nice contrast to all the sugary holiday fare!*

Melt butter in microwavable mixing bowl (cover top with paper towel to catch splatters); add other ingredients and form balls to place on greased cookie sheet. Bake for 10 minutes until cookies are just beginning to sizzle.

"We must have a pie. Stress cannot exist in the presence of a pie."
DAVID MAMET

Luscious Lime Pie

PREP TIME: 5 minutes
COOKING TIME: none, refrigerate
SERVES: 16 (8 per pie)

One of my mother's go-to desserts for unexpected company or days she simply ran out of time. She made them when she had a few minutes to spare and kept an extra in the freezer. Nobody would ever guess these refreshing pies take only 5 minutes to create.

1 (14 ounce) can sweetened condensed milk

1 (12 ounce) can frozen limeade, thawed (add 4 drops green food coloring to enhance greenness)

1 (13½ ounce) tub whipped topping (light okay)

2 ready-made graham cracker crusts

Garnish (such as thinly sliced limes or lemons, berries, or sprayed whipped cream florets)

Blend all ingredients (except garnish) together with electric mixer on medium-low; pour into graham cracker piecrusts and refrigerate or freeze (freezes beautifully). Thaw (if frozen) and top with garnish just before serving.

"Don't trust anyone who doesn't like chocolate."
DEBORA M. COTY,
CHOCOLATE GURU

53

Cookies & Cream Heaven

PREP TIME: 10 minutes
COOKING TIME: none, refrigerate
SERVES: 10 to 12

2 (4 ounce) boxes Cookies 'n' Cream instant pudding mix (may use sugar-free, fat-free pudding mix to save a few calories. Also, for a splash of color and twang of variety, I sometimes substitute two boxes of pistachio pudding mix. Yum!)

4 cups milk (for pudding; may use low fat but *not* skim)

1 (14 ounce) package Oreos (I use reduced fat to reduce guilt)

1 small bag mini marshmallows

1 (12 ounce) bag semisweet chocolate chips

8 ounces whipped topping (I use light)

Make pudding per box directions. Set aside. In large trifle dish or glass bowl, layer in this order: half each of crumbled Oreos (crush 3 to 4 cookies at a time by hand or crush them all together in large plastic bag), pudding, marshmallows, chocolate chips, whipped topping. Repeat layers, ending with whipped topping. Garnish with a few handfuls of crumbled Oreos. Refrigerate.

"Don't wreck a sublime chocolate experience by feeling guilty."
LORA BRODY

*A terrific munchy-
crunchy sweet snack
that's full of fiber.*

PREP TIME: 10 minutes
COOKING TIME: 3 minutes in microwave
SERVES: 10 to 12

3 cups Crispix cereal

3 cups Kix cereal

3 cups Multi-Grain Cheerios

3 cups Rice Chex

2 cups dry-roasted peanuts

2 cups pretzels (I like the small curly kind)

2 cups M&M's candy (plain or peanut)

20 ounces white chocolate baking squares (I like Eagle/Borden brand)

Pour all dry ingredients into jumbo mixing bowl and mix gently. Melt white chocolate in microwave per package directions and drizzle over dry ingredients. Stir until all particles are well coated. Spread out on nonstick cookie sheets or wax paper. When hard, store in airtight containers or ziplock bags.

Section 2

Soul-Fed

"A bagel is a doughnut with the sin removed."
GEORGE ROSENBAUM

How sweet are Your words to my taste,
sweeter than honey to my mouth!
PSALM 119:103 NKJV

Chuckle Break:
Satisfaction Guaranteed

My little mama is pretty much acknowledged by all who know her as one of the top ten cooks in the Deep South. None of this newfangled instant, microwavable, corner-cutting stuff for her, no siree. She still cooks the old-fashioned way, just like she learned from her mama growing up in rural north Georgia.

When she's expecting company, Mama spends all day preparing dinner, which in her opinion is incomplete without meat (she often has poor Daddy supervising spit-rotated pork roasting in the backyard), at least two vegetables (one green, one yellow for color balance), her famous mashed potatoes (more like a preview of heaven than a vegetable), bread with crockery butter, homemade strawberry jam, and freshly stewed tomatoes.

Then there's congealed salad (which isn't really considered fruit, salad, or dessert, although it's a conglomeration of all three), "real" salad (mixed greens/carrot salad/three-bean salad), and a huge bowl of fresh cut-up fruit. And, of course, a relish tray, consisting of three kinds of homemade pickles, various relishes, and deviled eggs.

Oh, we mustn't forget the smorgasbord of freshly baked pies and cakes. Mama considers it tacky if there aren't at least three dessert choices. And her hawk eye will be watching your plate to make sure you sample each and every one.

Yep, there's nothing quite like good ole soul food. . .comforts and satisfies the spirit, body, and emotions all at the same time. Many of the recipes in this section are Mama's, some passed down from her mama and grandma. Enjoy!

Southern Belle Fare

Grandma's Copper Pennies

✳Also known as "Sweet & Sour Carrots," this is one of the most colorful and delicious garden dishes ever. . . and good for you, to boot! Grandma always made it for family reunions and church covered dish dinners (no reheating needed).

PREP TIME: 15 minutes
COOKING TIME: 10 minutes on stove top
SERVES: 6 to 8

2 pounds carrots, washed (no need to peel)

1 bell pepper

1 medium onion

1 (10½ ounce) can condensed tomato soup

½ cup vinegar

½ cup oil

1 cup sugar

1 teaspoon dry mustard

1 teaspoon salt

1 teaspoon pepper

Slice carrots into "pennies"; cook until tender in unsalted water (I use a pressure cooker, but a microwave works well, too); drain and place in ungreased 2-quart casserole dish. Slice pepper and onion into ½-inch strips; add to carrots.

While carrots are cooking, make sweet & sour sauce by combining soup, vinegar, oil, sugar, and spices in a pot and bringing to a boil over medium-high heat, stirring occasionally. After boiling for 1 minute, remove from burner and pour over veggie mixture. Cover and refrigerate until ready to serve.

"The food in the South is as important as food anywhere because it defines a person's culture."
FANNIE FLAGG

Hot Chicken Salad

PREP TIME: 20 minutes
COOKING TIME: 20 to 25 minutes in preheated 350° oven
SERVES: 6 to 8

6 eggs

1 cup rice (2 cups cooked)

2 cups chopped cooked chicken

1 cup slivered almonds

1 cup mayonnaise (light okay)

2 (10½ ounce) cans cream of chicken soup

2 cups chopped celery

4 tablespoons lemon juice

4 tablespoons chopped onion

10 to 12 Ritz crackers, crushed

Boil eggs and cook rice (per package instructions) simultaneously; while they're cooking, combine remainder of ingredients (except crackers) in large mixing bowl. Add rice and eggs (peeled and cut into small pieces). Mix thoroughly; pour into greased 2-quart casserole dish. Top with crackers and bake for 20 to 25 minutes.

"There is no sight on earth more appealing than the sight of a woman making dinner for someone she loves."
THOMAS WOLFE

(I beg to differ with Mr. Wolfe. . . One thing is even better: a man making dinner for the woman he loves!)
DEBORA M. COTY

Mighty Pleasin' Potpie

PREP TIME: 15 minutes
COOKING TIME: 35 minutes in preheated 400° oven
SERVES: 4 to 6

✻A traditional Southern favorite with a few time-saving shortcuts; terrific way to transform leftover meat into a flavorful new dish.

1 (12 ounce) bag frozen mixed vegetables (microwavable in bag is best)

1 (10½ ounce) can cream of chicken soup

1 (10½ ounce) can cream of celery soup

1¼ cups chicken broth, or 1 (10½ ounce) can

4 cups cut-up cooked turkey, ham, chicken, or beef, or 2 (12 ounce) cans chunk chicken breast

2 ready-made refrigerated piecrusts

Cook vegetables per package directions. In 4-quart saucepan, heat soup, broth, and cooked vegetables to boiling, stirring constantly. Boil 1 minute; let simmer in juices a few additional minutes for softer vegetables. Add meat last.

Place bottom crust in greased pie plate or baking dish (1½ to 2 inches deep); pour in meat mixture. Place second piecrust on top and seal edges. Bake for 35 minutes or until golden brown.

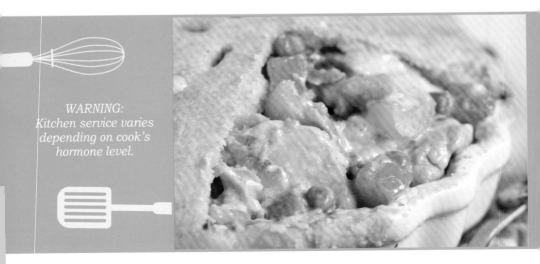

WARNING: Kitchen service varies depending on cook's hormone level.

Mimi's Blue Ribbon Chicken Gumbo

PREP TIME: 15 minutes
COOKING TIME: 30 minutes in preheated 350° oven
SERVES: 4 to 6

1 cup chopped cooked chicken ·

¾ cup mayonnaise (light okay)

1 cup cooked rice

¼ cup chopped celery

1 (10½ ounce) can cream of chicken soup

1 tablespoon onion flakes

1 tablespoon lemon juice

1 (5 ounce) can sliced water chestnuts, drained

Crushed potato chips

Combine all ingredients (except potato chips) in large mixing bowl. Pour into greased baking dish. May make up to a day ahead and refrigerate. When ready to cook, sprinkle a few handfuls of potato chips on top for a delightful salty crunch to augment the water chestnuts. Bake for 30 minutes or until piping hot.

"No one who cooks, cooks alone. . . she is surrounded by generations of cooks past."

LAURIE COLWIN

Scrumptious Shrimp & Grits

PREP TIME: 10 minutes
COOKING TIME: 15 minutes on stove top
SERVES: 6 to 8

4 cups chicken broth (I use fat free)

2 cups dry grits

1 teaspoon salt

3 cups milk (low fat okay)

2 pounds raw shrimp, peeled and deveined (fresh best but frozen okay)

2 tablespoons extra virgin olive oil

1 green bell pepper, cut into strips

1 red bell pepper, cut into strips

1 medium onion, cut into strips

2 tablespoons minced garlic

2 tablespoons Worcestershire sauce

2 cups shredded sharp cheddar cheese

Bring broth, grits, and salt to a boil in large saucepan with lid. Reduce heat to low and stir in milk; simmer covered until grits are thick (about 10 minutes), stirring frequently.

While grits are simmering, in large skillet sauté shrimp in olive oil with peppers, onion, and garlic until shrimp is pink and veggies are tender (8 to 10 minutes). Add Worcestershire sauce and continue stirring another 3 minutes over medium heat. (Tip: If you buy precooked shrimp like I sometimes do because they're on sale, sauté veggies until tender and then add cooked shrimp at the end just before pouring in Worcestershire sauce; if you sauté them too long, they'll get tough. You want to heat them, not recook them.)

"When baking, follow directions. When cooking, go by your own taste."
LAIKO BAHRS

Just before serving, mix cheese into grits until melted; grits should be creamy and light yellow. Serve shrimp mixture over cheese grits. (Tip: If the grits get done before your shrimp, you might need to add a little more milk to keep them from congealing; keep stirring them over low heat until you're ready to add the cheese and serve.)

Deb's Famous Chicken Salad

All modesty aside, it's true—people clamor for my special chicken salad. It's my claim to culinary fame. Well, that and my teriyaki pork (see Time-Wise section). I get requests all the time from family, friends, and sometimes people I don't even know, so here's my secret recipe so you can become famous, too!

PREP TIME: 15 minutes
COOKING TIME: none, served cold
SERVES: 6 to 8

2 cups cooked chicken, give or take (I use rotisserie leftovers or cook my own, see page 20)

½ to 1 medium onion (optional; quantity to your taste)

4 hard-boiled eggs, peeled

½ to 1 cup mayonnaise (Please don't hate me—these measurements are an estimate; I just add spoonfuls until it looks right. I use light mayo.)

2 hefty squirts honey mustard (about 2 tablespoons)

Salt and pepper to taste

¼ cup slivered almonds

½ to 1 cup green and/or red seedless grapes, quartered

Throw chicken, onion, and eggs in food processor; chop to your desired consistency. (Some like it really fine; others prefer coarsely chopped salad. If I'm making this for my son-in-law, I chop it by hand because he likes it chunky.) Transfer from food processor into medium mixing bowl; add mayonnaise, mustard, and salt and pepper. Mix well; it should be smooth but not squishy. Then stir in almonds. Last, add grapes (I prefer a mix of green and red because they're so perky) and fold gently into mixture. Serve on croissants or over a bed of mixed greens with sliced tomatoes. A real hit for girlfriend get-togethers or Bible study luncheons!

"Practice safe eating. Always use condiments."
UNKNOWN COOK

Breads

Chew Bread

PREP TIME: 10 minutes
COOKING TIME: 30 minutes in preheated 300° oven
SERVES: 8 to 10

1 stick (8 tablespoons) butter

1 pound brown sugar

2 cups flour (unbleached okay)

3 large eggs

4 teaspoons baking powder

1 teaspoon salt

✳ *My Alabama BFF, Julia, perfected this recipe, and I adore it. I could eat it all day long. This stuff is great to serve drop-in visitors and next-door neighbors. It freezes well, and I even like to eat it frozen (probably because once I see it I don't have enough patience to let it defrost).*

Start by melting butter in covered microwavable mixing bowl (about 1 minute on high). In same mixing bowl (saves dishwashing time), combine all ingredients and beat with electric mixer on medium-low until smooth (about 3 minutes). Pour into greased 3-quart baking pan (I like glass—seems to turn out better than in a metal pan). Bake for 30 minutes or until top is firm and toothpick comes out only slightly gooey. Cut into squares.

You may prefer yours less gooey than my fam (we like the inside pretty much the consistency of toothpaste); if so, bake for 5 to 7 additional minutes until toothpick comes out clean—it'll still be chewy, just not quite as gummy.

"If you're out of butter, use cream."
JULIA CHILD

Banana–Berry Loaf

PREP TIME: 15 minutes

COOKING TIME: 30 to 50 minutes in preheated 350° oven

SERVES: 10 to 12

1½ cups sugar

3 cups flour

4 large eggs

¾ cup oil

1 teaspoon baking soda

1½ teaspoons salt

4 to 5 very ripe bananas, mashed

¾ cup chopped walnuts or pecans

1 cup strawberry jam (*not* preserves, which are too chunky)

8 ounces sour cream (light okay)

Combine all ingredients in large mixing bowl (by hand or mixer). Pour into 2 large nonstick loaf pans or 5 nonstick mini loaf pans. Bake for 45 to 50 minutes (about 30 minutes for mini loaves) or until toothpick comes out clean. For a decadent breakfast, toast slices and serve warm with a pat of real butter melting on top. *Mmm.*

"All sorrows are less with bread."
MIGUEL DE CERVANTES SAAVEDRA

Parmesan Nuggets

PREP TIME: 10 minutes
COOKING TIME: 7 minutes in preheated 350° oven
SERVES: 8 to 10

✳Ultra simple and sure to be a hit with everyone you feed. My kids used to sneak handfuls of these delectable morsels before I could even get them to the table.

½ stick (4 tablespoons) butter

6 ounces grated Parmesan cheese

1 (10 ounce) can refrigerated biscuits (I like butter or buttermilk flavor)

Melt butter in covered microwavable bowl; fill another bowl with Parmesan cheese. Cut each biscuit into 4 quarters. Roll each small piece first in melted butter then in cheese until well coated. Place on ungreased cookie sheet and bake for 7 minutes until firm but not yet brown, watching to make sure they don't burn on bottom. I pop them in the oven as a lovely adjunct for breakfast, lunch, or dinner. Makes 40 bite-size cheese biscuits.

"A recipe has no soul. You, as the cook, must bring soul to the recipe."
THOMAS KELLER

A mouthwatering, heavenly smelling staple of Southern childhood.

Monkey Bread

PREP TIME: 20 minutes
COOKING TIME: 25 to 30 minutes in preheated 350° oven
SERVES: 6 to 8 (or just me)

2 tablespoons cinnamon

¼ cup sugar

4 (10 ounce) cans refrigerated biscuits

½ cup raisins (optional)

½ cup chopped walnuts or pecans (optional)

1 stick (8 tablespoons) butter

1 cup brown sugar

Mix cinnamon and sugar together in plastic bag. Cut biscuits in quarters; drop pieces in bag and shake until coated with cinnamon sugar. Layer pieces in greased Bundt pan, interspersing raisins and nuts as you go. Melt butter in small saucepan over medium-high heat; add brown sugar and boil for 1 minute (I add the leftover cinnamon sugar after removing pan from burner). Pour evenly over biscuits. Bake for 25 to 30 minutes until dough is firm. Turn out of pan immediately. Just see if you can keep your little monkey paws off this awesome stuff long enough to serve to guests. Wear a bib and be prepared to lick your fingers.

"Humor keeps us alive. Humor and food. Don't forget food. You can go a week without laughing."
JOSS WHEDON

Shrimp Pizza Bites

PREP TIME: 15 minutes
COOKING TIME: 5 to 10 minutes in preheated 400° oven
SERVES: 10 to 12

＊My dear mother-in-law's favorite finger food to serve at parties. Now it's mine, too! Easy to make ahead and freeze until time to heat and serve.

6 English muffins

1 stick (8 tablespoons) butter, softened

5 ounces sharp cheddar cheese spread

1 (6 ounce) can tiny shrimp

¼ teaspoon garlic salt

¼ teaspoon seasoned salt (I use Lowry's)

With serrated knife, split muffins into 12 halves. Spread layer of butter then layer of cheese on each muffin half. Add shrimp and gently press into cheese (so they don't fall off). Liberally sprinkle garlic salt and seasoned salt on top. With serrated knife, cut each muffin half into 8 triangles (like a teensy pizza). Place pieces on ungreased cookie sheet and either bake for 5 to 8 minutes to serve immediately or, if you're planning to serve them another day, cover tightly with plastic wrap and freeze. Mom Coty froze them in ziplock bags, but I find the pieces stay intact better (the little shrimpies like to fall off) by freezing them directly on the cookie sheet. When ready to bake, remove plastic wrap and place on counter for 10 to 15 minutes; bake 8 to 10 minutes or until light brown on top. Best served warm, but people will scarf them up cold, too. Makes 96 pieces.

"People who love to eat are always the best people."
JULIA CHILD

Harvest Bread

PREP TIME: 15 minutes
COOKING TIME: 40 to 50 minutes in preheated 350° oven
SERVES: 6 to 8

1½ cups sugar

½ cup oil

2 eggs

1 (8 ounce) can pumpkin

1 cup flour

1 cup oats

1 teaspoon baking powder

1 tablespoon allspice

2 teaspoons cinnamon

1 teaspoon salt

1 teaspoon nutmeg

¼ cup raisins

½ cup chopped pecans or walnuts (optional)

Combine sugar, oil, eggs, and pumpkin in large mixing bowl; add dry ingredients, raisins, and nuts last. Pour into greased loaf pan (batter will be thick). Bake for 40 to 50 minutes until toothpick comes out clean.

Chuckle Break:
Lumps and All

*My writer friend Sharron Cosby shared this LOL story with me, and I wanted it to brighten your day as much as it did mine:

My future in-laws were coming for Sunday lunch. I decided to fix a roast, mashed potatoes, green beans, and store-bought rolls. How difficult could that Southern-standard meal be?

The roast came out of the oven fork tender. The green beans and potatoes looked and smelled scrumptious. My challenge: roast gravy.

I had never fixed gravy, but I'd watched my mother prepare it many times. *This should be a cinch,* I boasted to myself. I knew she used something in a yellow box and mixed it with some water. I grabbed the first yellow box I saw—Arm & Hammer Baking Soda—and spooned some into a coffee cup, just like Mother did. I added the water and stirred until dissolved.

Mother also stirred flour into the roast drippings. I sprinkled flour into the pan and stirred until it became a paste. Next, I added the baking soda water. There was an immediate chemical reaction. The flour started bubbling and foaming, and it formed a big glob in the center of the pan. I added more water. More bubbles. I stirred and

stirred, hoping the blob would dissipate.

I grabbed a fork and started smashing the lumps like a wild woman. My mother-in-law was coming, for Pete's sake, and I wanted her to know I could properly feed her son. My sweet man, bless his heart, took over mashing the lumpy concoction, while assuring me all would be fine. The more he mashed, the bigger the lumps grew.

God's favor rested on me when Danny's parents called to tell us they couldn't stop for lunch after all. I breathed a sigh of relief that my baking soda gravy would be a closely held secret.

I fixed our plates, and Danny cleaned his, including the gravy. He teased me that he had never had gravy with a built-in burp preventer. It must not have been too bad. We recently celebrated forty years of marriage.

"I come from a home where gravy is a beverage."
ERMA BOMBECK

Munchies

Strawberry Pizza

PREP TIME: 10 minutes
COOKING TIME: 15 minutes in preheated 375° oven
SERVES: 6 to 8

CRUST:

2 cups flour

2 sticks (1 cup) butter, melted

½ cup powdered sugar

SAUCE:

6 ounces cream cheese, softened

1 cup powdered sugar

8 ounces whipped topping

TOPPING:

1 quart fresh strawberries

8 ounces strawberry glaze

Mix crust ingredients and form ball. Spread dough ball on greased pizza pan or 9x13-inch baking pan. Bake for 15 minutes; remove cookie crust from oven and let cool. Combine sauce ingredients with electric mixer and spread on cooled cookie crust. Wash and slice strawberries; gently blend with glaze and spread on top of cream cheese mixture.

"Diet, schmiet. Listen, if you're going to cheat on your husband, don't pick an ugly man."
DEBORA M. COTY, FROM *TOO BLESSED TO BE STRESSED*

Puppy Chow

PREP TIME: 15 minutes
COOKING TIME: 5 to 8 minutes on stove top
SERVES: 12 to 15

1 (12 ounce) box Rice Chex

1 (15 ounce) box raisins

1 (16 ounce) can peanuts

2 sticks (1 cup) butter

12 ounces semisweet chocolate chips

1 cup creamy peanut butter

1 pound powdered sugar

Mix Chex, raisins, and peanuts in a *very* large bowl. (Your bathtub would work.) I use a soup vat. Melt butter and chocolate chips in a saucepan over medium heat; when melted, add peanut butter and stir until smooth. Pour over dry ingredients and mix until all particles are coated.

Then the snow part: Spoon chow into large brown paper bag containing half the powdered sugar. Fold down top and gently shake upside down and right side up again until puppy chow is coated white (it may be a bit clumpy at this point). Remove batch and repeat. Keep adding sugar to bag as needed and repeat until all puppy chow is coated. Spread on cookie sheets or counter covered in wax paper to set. Try not to stuff your face. Store in airtight containers or gallon-size ziplock bags. Freezes well.

"You only live once. Lick the bowl."
WISE WOMAN IN THE BAKING AISLE

Chocolate Brickle

PREP TIME: 5 minutes
COOKING TIME: 15 minutes in preheated 350° oven
SERVES: 8 to 10 (or just me if nobody's watching)

✳This incredibly easy-to-make stuff is to die for! You will not believe how exquisite the combination of sweet, salty, and buttery can be until you've tried it. And then you're hooked. Affectionately known as Chocolate Crack (because you can't stop eating it), I'm including two variations—one brickle, one toffee—that will start feeding your addiction.

1 stick (8 tablespoons) salted butter (use real butter!)

¼ cup sugar

1 teaspoon vanilla

1 sleeve saltine crackers

12 ounces chocolate chips or chocolate melting wafers (I prefer wafers found in the cake decorating aisle; semisweet chocolate chips work, too, but tend to melt a little lumpy and need more flattening to produce a smooth surface.)

½ cup chopped walnuts or pecans (optional)

Melt butter (approximately 1 minute on high) in small covered microwavable bowl (I use a 4-cup glass measuring cup covered with a paper towel to catch splatters); stir in sugar and vanilla. Microwave again for 1 minute on high until boiling.

Line 9x13-inch baking dish with aluminum foil and coat foil with cooking spray; cover with single layer of saltines, breaking as needed to cover entire bottom. Pour butter mixture over crackers evenly. Bake for 8 minutes (this allows crackers to soak up butter and crisp up a bit).

Remove pan from oven; sprinkle chocolate chips or wafers over crackers and return to oven for 7 minutes or until chocolate is melted. Remove from oven; using the back side of a large spoon coated with cooking spray, spread chocolate evenly (flatten out bumps). Sprinkle on nuts if desired (gently press into chocolate so they won't fall off). Refrigerate and, when hard, remove from pan and peel foil away; break into small pieces. Brickle freezes wonderfully; in fact, I actually prefer to nibble it frozen. And nibble. And nibble. And nibble.

To Die For Toffee

PREP TIME: 10 minutes
COOKING TIME: 5 minutes on stove top + 10 minutes in preheated 350° oven
SERVES: 8 to 10

1 (14 ounce) box graham crackers

1 stick (8 tablespoons) salted butter

½ cup brown sugar

12 ounces semisweet chocolate chips

Sea salt

Line 9x13-inch baking dish with aluminum foil; coat foil with cooking spray. Cover bottom with single layer of graham crackers, breaking to fit. In saucepan, combine butter with brown sugar and bring to a boil over medium-high heat, stirring constantly. Boil for 5 minutes, still stirring constantly, to create toffee (warning: if you stop stirring, it may burn). Pour toffee over graham crackers and bake for 10 minutes (check to make sure bottoms don't burn). Remove pan from oven and sprinkle chocolate chips over top. Wait a few minutes for chips to melt, then spread out evenly; finish with a light sprinkling of sea salt. Cool in refrigerator; when hard, remove from pan and peel foil from toffee; break into small pieces.

"A balanced diet is a cookie in each hand."
BARBARA JOHNSON

Guess Again Cookie Bars

PREP TIME: 10 minutes
COOKING TIME: 15 to 20 minutes in preheated 350° oven
SERVES: 10 to 12

✳I adore these versatile cookie bars that originated with Lila Rae Yawn, mother of my hometown friend, Dianne. Tailor the ingredients to your eaters—add granola, omit coconut, change flavors of chocolate. . . hey, you can't go wrong!

2 sticks (1 cup) butter, softened

1 cup sugar

1 cup brown sugar

1 teaspoon vanilla

2 eggs

2½ cups flour

2 teaspoons baking soda

½ teaspoon baking powder

½ teaspoon salt

2 cups oats

PICK ONE: 2 cups Rice Krispies OR granola (I use Cascadian Farm organic maple brown sugar granola cereal)

PICK ONE: 1 cup peanut butter chips OR butterscotch chips

PICK ONE: 1 cup semisweet chocolate chips OR dark chocolate chips

PICK ONE: 1 cup coconut OR chopped walnuts OR chopped pecans

Cream together butter, sugars, vanilla, and eggs. Add flour, baking soda, baking powder, salt, and oats; mix until well blended. Now it's time to be creative! Choose ingredients to accessorize your basic cookie and mix well. Using the back side of a wet spoon, spread batter (it will be thick) in greased 9x13-inch baking pan and bake for 15 to 20 minutes until slightly brown on top and toothpick comes out clean (I opt for 15 minutes because I like mine a smidge gooey). P.S. You can use batter for drop cookies, too (just bake for 10 minutes).

"As for butter versus margarine, I trust cows more than chemists."
JOAN GUSSOW

Sweethearts

PREP TIME: 10 minutes
COOKING TIME: none, refrigerate
SERVES: 8 to 10

12 ounces milk chocolate chips

1 cup creamy peanut butter

1 cup peanut butter chips

3 cups Corn Flakes

Melt chocolate chips in microwavable mixing bowl on high for 2 minutes, stirring every 30 seconds. Stir in peanut butter until well blended, then add peanut butter chips (chips don't need to melt). Lightly crush Corn Flakes by the handful as you drop them into mixing bowl; gently fold into chocolate mixture. Scoop by the tablespoon onto cookie sheet lined with wax paper (run a damp sponge over cookie sheet to anchor wax paper). Refrigerate until firm.

"Chocolate should be considered a vegetable. It is, after all, derived from cocoa beans."
DEBORA M. COTY, FROM *MOM NEEDS CHOCOLATE*

79

Oooey Gooey Brownies

PREP TIME: 5 minutes
COOKING TIME: 15 minutes in preheated 350° oven
SERVES: 6 to 8

✻ *My friend Sandi shared this bodacious homemade brownie recipe with me thirty-five years ago when we were each newlyweds. In case of hormonal chocolate sniper attacks, it can be ready within 20 minutes. I'm pretty sure it's the reason we're both still married.*

1 cup shortening

½ cup baking cocoa

1½ cups sugar

1½ cups self-rising flour

2 large eggs

1 teaspoon vanilla

1 cup pecans or walnuts, chopped (optional)

FUDGE GLAZE:

2 cups powdered sugar

1 tablespoon baking cocoa

1 tablespoon milk (add more a few drops at a time to achieve glaze consistency)

In large saucepan, melt shortening over medium-high heat, then reduce to low and add remaining brownie ingredients while still on burner. Stir until well blended. Pour into greased 8x8-inch baking pan. Bake for 15 minutes.

Mix together fudge glaze ingredients. While brownies are hot, pour on glaze. Let cool; glaze will harden as brownies cool, but you can enjoy it gooey if you can't wait.

"Baklava is the reason there's no peace in the Middle East. Israelis say it's their recipe, Syrians claim it's theirs; chefs in Jordan and Lebanon insist they developed it."
ARDYTHE KOLLO

Tip: If you don't have self-rising flour, just use regular flour + 1 teaspoon baking powder.

Comment: I don't know why it doesn't work the same to use liquid cooking oil if you're going to melt the shortening anyway, but I tried it and it doesn't. Stick with shortening.

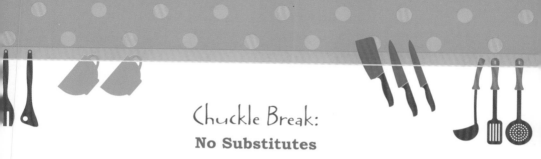

Chuckle Break:
No Substitutes

"I've heard of green eggs and ham, but this is ridiculous!" my daughter whispered at the Thanksgiving table.

She was referring to the huge, nearly untouched dish of what was supposed to be sweet potato casserole. Topped with a delicious mixture of chopped pecans, coconut, and brown sugar, creamed sweet potatoes were a favorite at our family holiday celebrations.

But something was definitely amiss. Instead of their usually inviting orange-y sweetness, the potatoes were pea green. My sister, the chronically distracted cook, had reached into the cabinet for vanilla extract and grabbed the similarly shaped bottle of green food coloring instead.

By the time she'd realized her mistake, it was too late. *Well, they may look different, but they'll taste the same,* she reasoned as she popped the casserole dish in the oven.

But it just didn't work that way. No one could bring themselves to scoop the sickly green grub onto their plates. We just couldn't wrap our heads—or appetites—around a substitute for the real thing.

I had a similar experience while hosting a dinner party. In a quandary about what to serve for dessert, I settled on a low-calorie

pie recipe that looked simply scrumptious in the photo. All the regular cheesecake ingredients had been replaced with fat-free, sugar-free substitutes, topped with fat-free whipped topping and drizzled with zero-calorie faux chocolate sauce.

It turned out gorgeous! I was so proud to be serving my guests such a masterpiece that wouldn't add more wattle to their waddles.

At the first bite, I saw the faces all around me fall. It tasted like soggy cardboard. Magazine-cover beautiful it might have been, but there's no substitute for the real thing.

Faith can be like that. Many religions look tempting on the outside, but once you get past the fluffy frosting, you find the ingredients have no real substance. They're inferior. Flat. Fake.

Jesus made it very clear that true faith is found only through Him. He, Himself, *is* truth. And the *only* way to a living, breathing, dynamic relationship with God is through Jesus. Everything else is just a poor substitute for the real thing.

As worthless in the end as green sweet potatoes and faux cheesecake.

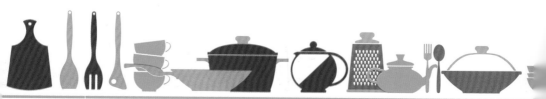

Banana Pudding

PREP TIME: 10 minutes
COOKING TIME: 15 to 20 minutes in preheated 350° oven
SERVES: 6 to 8

3 large eggs at room temperature, separated

½ cup sugar

1 cup milk (low fat okay)

1 tablespoon flour

1 teaspoon vanilla

1 (12 ounce) box vanilla wafers

3 to 4 ripe bananas

2 tablespoons sugar (for meringue)

In saucepan, combine egg yolks (save whites for meringue) and sugar; add milk and flour. Cook over medium-low heat until thickened, stirring frequently. Add vanilla. In 2-quart serving bowl, layer vanilla wafers and bananas twice, ending with wafers on top. Pour pudding over wafers and bananas. To make meringue, beat egg whites and 2 tablespoons sugar with electric mixer on high until stiff. Spoon meringue on top of pudding, creating pretty little peaks. Bake for 15 to 20 minutes until peaks of meringue are slightly browned (watch it carefully; once it starts browning, meringue burns before you know it). Let stand at least 10 minutes before serving. Refrigerate leftovers. (I prefer it cold).

Seize life! Eat bread with gusto, drink wine with a robust heart. Oh yes—God takes pleasure in your pleasure!
ECCLESIASTES 9:7 MSG

Apple Fries

PREP TIME: 10 minutes
COOKING TIME: 10 to 12 minutes in preheated 350°
oven
SERVES: 8 to 10

1 (21 ounce) can apple pie filling

2 ready-made refrigerated piecrusts (I go with Pillsbury)

1 medium egg

Caramel fruit dip (found in produce section of grocery stores)

Puree pie filling in blender, food processor, or electric mixer to the consistency of thick applesauce (and to answer your next question, no, real applesauce won't work, so stick with pie filling). Unroll 1 piecrust onto a cutting board sprinkled lightly with flour (so dough won't stick). Spread pie filling on dough, leaving a ½-inch border around edge for squish spillage. Cover with second piecrust and press lightly, like an applesauce sandwich.

Make an egg wash by whisking egg in a bowl with ½ teaspoon water. Brush egg wash on top piecrust for a shiny finish. Using pizza cutter, cut dough into strips the size of french fries, about ½ inch wide and 3 inches long (makes approximately 30 fries).

With spatula, place apple fries on greased baking sheet and bake for 10 to 12 minutes, until firm and just beginning to turn golden brown (not too brown). Wait at least 5 minutes until cool and serve with caramel dip.

"Condensed milk is wonderful. I don't see how they can get a cow to sit down on those little cans."
FRED ALLEN

Mudbar Ecstasy

PREP TIME: 10 minutes
COOKING TIME: 20 minutes in preheated 375° oven
SERVES: 6 to 8

¾ cup brown sugar

1 stick (8 tablespoons) butter, softened

1 large egg

1 teaspoon vanilla

1 cup flour

½ teaspoon salt

½ teaspoon baking soda

12 ounces semisweet chocolate chips, divided

½ cup walnuts or pecans, chopped (optional)

With electric mixer, beat brown sugar, butter, egg, and vanilla until creamy. Add flour, salt, and baking soda. Last, stir in chocolate chips and nuts (if desired), saving ⅔ cup chocolate chips for later. Pour into greased 8x8-inch baking pan. Bake for 20 minutes. While piping hot from oven, sprinkle remainder of chocolate chips on top. When shiny, spread evenly over top. Let cool and cut into bars. Refrigerate or not (I like them cold!).

"I suffer from CDD: Chocolate Deficit Disorder. My medication is a choco-infusion every few hours to maintain temperament stability and the mental health of those around me."
DEBORA M. COTY, FROM *TOO BLESSED TO BE STRESSED*

Blueberry Delight

PREP TIME: 10 minutes
COOKING TIME: none, refrigerate
SERVES: 6 to 8

1 (14 ounce) box graham crackers

1 large box or 2 small boxes vanilla instant pudding mix

3 cups milk (low fat okay; for pudding)

8 ounces whipped topping

1 (21 ounce) can blueberry pie filling

Line greased 9x13-inch pan with whole graham crackers, breaking as necessary to fit bottom of pan. Prepare pudding per package directions and allow to set for 2 to 3 minutes. When thickened, fold in whipped topping. Spread layer of pudding over graham crackers, then repeat layers, ending with graham crackers on top. Spread pie filling over top layer of crackers. Chill and serve.

Section 3

Heart-Healthy

"Vegetables are a must on a diet. I suggest carrot cake, zucchini bread, and pumpkin pie."
JIM DAVIS

When you have eaten and are satisfied, praise the LORD your God for the good land he has given you.
DEUTERONOMY 8:10 NIV

Low Fat

Greek-Style Orzo Chicken Salad

✳ My friend Pat's phenomenal recipe; perfect for leftover rotisserie or grilled chicken. May be prepared the day before and can be served either warm or cold.

PREP TIME: 15 minutes
COOKING TIME: 10 minutes on stove top
SERVES: 4 to 6

8 ounces orzo (pasta shaped like rice)

1 tablespoon lemon juice

1 tablespoon red wine vinegar

Seasonings: 1 tablespoon deli-style mustard, ½ teaspoon salt, ½ teaspoon pepper, 1 teaspoon dried oregano (fresh is even better), 1 teaspoon dill

⅓ cup olive oil

4 scallions, including green tops, chopped fine

½ cup black olives, pitted and sliced in half (easy to remove for non-olive eaters)

2 to 4 cooked chicken breasts, cubed (or you may substitute cooked shrimp)

Cherry tomatoes, halved; or 1 medium tomato, chopped

4 ounces feta cheese, crumbled

½ cup chopped cucumber (optional)

Cook orzo per box directions; rinse and drain. In large bowl, whisk together lemon juice, vinegar, and seasonings. Add oil slowly and stir. Then stir in orzo, scallions, and olives; toss lightly.

Prior to serving, top with chicken, tomatoes, feta cheese, and, if desired, cucumbers. If made ahead and refrigerated, you can add chicken early but reserve cukes, tomatoes, and feta to include right before serving.

"Part of the secret of success in life is to eat what you like and let the food fight it out inside."
MARK TWAIN

Delicious Fish Fillets

✳I almost didn't include my friend Marlene's recipe because it's so simple it doesn't even seem like a recipe. But I know you'll adore it as much as I do, so here it is. . .a highly nutritious fish dish in merely 10 minutes.

PREP TIME: 2 minutes
COOKING TIME: 8 minutes on stove top
SERVES: 4

1 tablespoon extra virgin olive oil (it won't smoke)

1 heaping teaspoon minced garlic

4 boneless fillets of your favorite fish, fresh or frozen/thawed (I like tilapia)

2 tablespoons lemon juice

Seasoning (I recommend McCormick Grill Mates Roasted Garlic & Herb)

Pour olive oil in frying pan over medium heat; add garlic and spread around pan. Run fish through lemon juice to coat each side. Place fillet in pan; cook for 5 minutes, using spatula to gently nudge fish so it won't stick. Turn fish over and sprinkle with seasoning. Cook another 3 minutes until fillet flakes with fork. Serve hot and tasty.

"Fish is the only food that is considered spoiled once it smells like what it is."
P. J. O'ROURKE

Best Bean Soup Ever

PREP TIME: 10 minutes
COOKING TIME: 15 minutes on stove top
SERVES: 6 to 8

✳This low-fat selection couldn't be easier—you basically dump everything into a pot and stir. Tastes great in only 25 minutes, start to finish. A culinary marvel!

1 large onion, chopped

1 teaspoon garlic powder

1 (15 ounce) can pinto beans

1 (15 ounce) can kidney beans

2 cups fat-free chicken broth

½ cup ketchup

1 (15 ounce) can diced tomatoes (optional)

1 teaspoon cumin

1 cup instant rice (white or brown)

1 (15 ounce) can refried beans (fat free okay)

Sauté onion and garlic over medium-high heat until tender (I use a nonstick pan and several squirts of Parkay Spray vegetable oil spread, which has zero trans fat and cholesterol). Add to other ingredients (except raw rice and refried beans) in soup pot; heat to near-boiling. Reduce heat, then stir in rice and simmer for 5 minutes until rice plumps up. If soup seems too thick, add a little water (rice sucks up a lot of liquid). Last, stir in refried beans until well blended. Serve in feed buckets with shovels (because that's how fast your family will down this hearty soup!).

"Soup is liquid comfort."
UNKNOWN (BUT SOUNDS A
LOT LIKE MY GRANNY)

Chuckle Break:
Martha's Meatloaf

*A culinary gem from my writing bud, Martha Bolton.

Meat, as much as needed
Bread crumbs, equal parts to meat

Mix all ingredients and bake. Meatloaf is done when
knife cannot penetrate it. Yields one small patio.

Cures Anything Chicken–Veggie Soup

PREP TIME: 10 minutes
COOKING TIME: 15 minutes on stove top
SERVES: 6 to 8

✱I like to customize this soup by dumping into the pot any vegetable or pasta leftovers I find in my fridge. Turns out marvelously different every time!

2 cups chopped cooked chicken

4 cups fat-free chicken broth

4 chicken bouillon cubes

1 medium onion, chopped

1 (15 ounce) can mixed vegetables

1 (15 ounce) can garbanzo beans

1 (15 ounce) can whole kernel corn

1 (4 ounce) can mushrooms (optional)

1 (8½ ounce) can sweet green peas or lima beans (or both)

1 tablespoon minced garlic

1 teaspoon parsley (fresh or dried)

1 (3 ounce) package chicken flavor Ramen noodles

1 cup instant rice (white or brown)

Start by cooking chicken overnight ahead of time as described on page 20. (Or you can use canned or leftover rotisserie chicken.) Pour chicken broth and bouillon cubes into large soup pot over medium-high heat. Dump in onion, canned vegetables (including water in cans), and seasonings; then last, add rice and Ramen noodles (be sure to include Ramen flavoring). When near-boiling, reduce heat and simmer for 10 minutes, stirring occasionally. If soup is too thick once rice and noodles plump up, add a little more water.

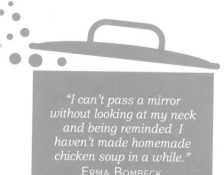

"I can't pass a mirror without looking at my neck and being reminded I haven't made homemade chicken soup in a while."
ERMA BOMBECK

Sweet & Sour Vegetable Salad

PREP TIME: 15 minutes (make a day ahead and refrigerate)
COOKING TIME: 5 minutes on stove top
SERVESS: 8 to 10

1 cup apple cider vinegar

1¼ cups sugar

1 (8½ ounce) can sweet green peas, drained

1 (15 ounce) can seasoned green beans, drained

1 (15 ounce) can chow mein vegetables

1 (4 ounce) can sliced mushrooms, drained

1 (8 ounce) can sliced water chestnuts

2 cups bean sprouts

1 small jar pimientos, drained

1 large onion, chopped

3 stalks celery, chopped

1 red bell pepper, sliced (optional)

To make sauce, in small saucepan, combine vinegar and sugar; bring to a boil for 1 minute. Mix vegetables together in large mixing bowl; drain off excess liquid. Pour sauce over veggies and mix well. Chill in refrigerator overnight.

"I like a cook who smiles out loud when he tastes his own work. Let God worry about your modesty; I want to see your enthusiasm."
ROBERT FARAR CAPON

Veggie and Rice Sauté

PREP TIME: 10 minutes
COOKING TIME: 15 minutes on stove top
SERVES: 4

4 tablespoons Earth Balance buttery spread or extra virgin olive oil

5 cups of a variety of your favorite veggies, including at least one dark leafy green like spinach, bok choy, or swiss chard (two are even better!). May include carrots, onions, peppers, tomatoes, broccoli, cauliflower, peas, beans. . .you name it!

Oregano to taste

3 cups cooked whole grain brown rice or 3 cups cooked rotini pasta

Melt spread (or heat olive oil) in large skillet over medium heat (may need to add more depending on how much liquid your veggies produce). Add dense veggies that take longer to cook first (such as onions, carrots, or peppers). Sprinkle with oregano; stir and cover, letting vegetables steam and simmer for about 5 minutes. Now put in softer veggies like broccoli and leafy greens. Add a little more oregano (to taste) and simmer for another 5 minutes, stirring occasionally. When veggies look tender (don't overcook!), serve over rice or pasta and enjoy.

Fiber Rich

No Yeast Whole Wheat Bread

PREP TIME: 15 minutes
COOKING TIME: 50 minutes in preheated 375° oven
SERVES: 4 to 6

1 egg

⅓ cup brown sugar

3 teaspoons honey

1 teaspoon baking soda

1½ teaspoons melted butter

2 cups whole wheat flour

1 teaspoon salt

2 cups milk (low fat okay)

½ cup walnuts or pecans, finely chopped (optional)

Combine egg, sugar, honey, and baking soda in mixing bowl; beat with electric mixer on low for 1 minute. Gradually add other ingredients to mixing bowl (nuts go in last), increasing mixing speed to medium as needed to mix thoroughly. Place in greased loaf pan and bake for 50 minutes until toothpick comes out clean.

"Do pasta and antipasto served in the same meal cancel each other out?"
DEBORA M. COTY, FROM *FEAR, FAITH, AND A FISTFUL OF CHOCOLATE*

Wild & Crazy Chicken & Rice

PREP TIME: 15 minutes
COOKING TIME: 10 minutes on stove top
SERVES: 6

1 cup uncooked wild rice

2 cups cubed cooked chicken breasts

1½ cups halved green grapes (can use red seedless, too)

1 cup sliced water chestnuts, drained

¾ cup low-fat mayonnaise

1 cup cashews (optional)

Lettuce or spinach leaves for serving

Cook rice per package directions (sprinkle on a little seasoned salt if desired). Remove from burner and let cool to room temperature (about 10 minutes). While rice is cooling, combine remainder of ingredients (except cashews) in bowl. Add cooled rice and gently fold together. Cover and refrigerate. Just before serving, add cashews so they're nice and crunchy. Serve over lettuce or spinach leaves. Awesome paired with No Yeast Whole Wheat Bread (page 99) and a colorful slice of fruit.

"The two most important kitchen utensils are attached to your arms. . . get in there, get your fingers dirty!"
RACHEL RAY

Keep You Full Breakfast Bowl

PREP TIME: 10 minutes
COOKING TIME: none
SERVES: 2 (easily doubled for 4)

1 cup quick oats

2 tablespoons currants (or other dried fruit)

2 tablespoons pecan pieces

4 tablespoons chopped fresh fruit (bananas, apples, pears, or peaches are lovely)

1 teaspoon brown sugar (optional)

1 cup milk (may opt for almond milk for dairy free)

Place oats in bowl; add currants, pecans, and fresh fruit. Sprinkle with brown sugar if desired. Add milk last. Enjoy!

Cold weather variation: Try it hot; instead of adding milk at end, add boiling water to your preferred consistency and cover bowl with plate for 3 to 5 minutes until water is absorbed. Drizzle with a little milk to keep it creamy.

"Kitchen happiness all depends on how you handle plan B."
UNKNOWN (BUT SHOULD HAVE BEEN ME)

Great Munchin' Granola

PREP TIME: 10 minutes
COOKING TIME: 15 minutes in preheated 325° oven
SERVES: a small army (makes a LOT but freezes well)

✳ My little mister and kids ate their weights in this wonderful stuff over the years. Toted around in ziplock bags, you couldn't beat it for economy, taste, and nutrition!

1 cup safflower or canola oil

1½ cups honey

7 cups oats

1 cup soybeans

½ cup sesame seeds (hull on)

¾ cup raw pumpkin seeds

1 cup sunflower seeds

½ cup wheat germ

1½ cups chopped walnuts

½ cup bran

½ cup raisins

1 cup coconut (optional)

Heat oil and honey together in small pot over medium heat. Combine all dry ingredients in very large mixing bowl (I use a jumbo soup pot). Pour oil/honey over dry mixture and combine with large spoon until all particles are coated. Spread onto baking sheets (with sides so granola won't fall off in your oven) and bake for 15 minutes, stirring twice (you can clump it a bit on the baking sheets and it will dry nicely without burning; if you spread it out thin, you'll go through every cookie sheet on your block).

"Nutritionally sound diets avoid creating waist baskets."
DEBORA M. COTY,
FROM *TOO BLESSED TO BE STRESSED*

Hearty 4-Bean Salad

PREP TIME: 15 minutes
COOKING TIME: none, refrigerate
SERVES: 6 to 8

2 (15 ounce) cans garbanzo beans (chickpeas), rinsed

1 (15 ounce) can dark red kidney beans, rinsed

1 (15 ounce) can light red kidney beans, rinsed

2 (15 ounce) cans black beans, unrinsed

1 cup chopped bell pepper

1 cup chopped celery

1 cup thinly sliced raw carrots

½ cup chopped onion

1 bottle of your favorite Italian dressing

Salt and pepper to taste

Combine all beans in large bowl. Add bell pepper, celery, carrots, and onion; stir well. Pour on Italian dressing gradually, to your preference of thickness. Add salt and pepper.

"Ordinary folk prefer familiar tastes. . .but a gourmet would sample a fried park bench just to know how it tastes."
WALTER MOERS

Eggplant Supreme

✳ *My great-aunt's recipe. She was the queen of unique vegetable dishes.*

PREP TIME: 15 minutes
COOKING TIME: 20 minutes in preheated 350° oven
SERVES: 6 to 8

1 large eggplant, peeled and cubed

½ medium onion, chopped

⅓ cup sliced green bell peppers

2 tablespoons butter

1 cup sliced mushrooms (fresh or canned)

2 tablespoons flour

½ cup milk (low fat okay)

3 teaspoons chopped pimientos

½ cup bacon bits

Salt and pepper to taste

⅓ cup Italian-style bread crumbs

⅓ cup grated Parmesan cheese

Boil cubed eggplant in water for 10 minutes (or cook in microwave); while it's cooking, sauté onion and green pepper in 12-inch skillet until tender (sauté in butter and you won't have to add it later). Add mushrooms, flour, milk, pimientos, bacon bits, salt and pepper; simmer for 5 minutes, stirring frequently. When eggplant is soft, drain water and add eggplant to other ingredients in skillet; mix together and simmer another 2 to 3 minutes. Spoon mixture into greased 1½-quart baking dish; top with bread crumbs and cheese. Bake for 20 minutes until cheese has melted and casserole is set.

"We all need self-discipline. You don't simply wish for dinner and then sit back and wait for it to magically appear, do you? Well, come to think of it, sometimes I do. . .but you shouldn't. You plan your menu, do the shopping, prepare the food, and then pop it in the oven. Otherwise you'll end up with a growling tummy and empty plate. It's exactly the same for spiritual nourishment. Planning, preparation, and actually doing something to feed our souls are what keep our faith alive and healthy."
DEBORA M. COTY, FROM *MORE BEAUTY, LESS BEAST*

Vegetarian

California Cuisine

PREP TIME: 10 minutes
COOKING TIME: none, refrigerate
SERVES: 4 to 6

¼ cup red wine vinegar

¼ cup olive oil

½ teaspoon minced garlic

1 cup chopped plum tomatoes

½ cup chopped fresh parsley

1 (11 ounce) can shoepeg corn, drained (may use kernel corn)

1 (15 ounce) can black-eyed peas, rinsed

2 avocados, diced

½ cup golden raisins

½ cup chopped green onion

1 teaspoon cumin

To make dressing, whisk together vinegar, olive oil, and garlic; in separate serving bowl, mix together all other ingredients. Pour dressing over veggies and toss lightly. Chill before serving to blend and maximize flavors.

"Food is symbolic of love when words are inadequate."
ALAN D. WOLFELT

Sweet Potato Home Fries

PREP TIME: 10 minutes
COOKING TIME: 25 minutes in preheated 400° oven
SERVES: 6 to 8 (easily doubled or even tripled)

4 sweet potatoes

4 tablespoons extra virgin olive oil

¼ teaspoon pepper

¼ teaspoon garlic powder

½ teaspoon seasoning salt

Wash and slice sweet potatoes lengthwise (leave skins on). Pour olive oil in small bowl and toss potato slices until well coated; sprinkle liberally with seasonings and spread on nonstick cookie sheet. Bake for 25 minutes until potatoes are soft.

The righteous eat to their hearts' content, but the stomach of the wicked goes hungry.
PROVERBS 13:25 NIV

Pasta Salad Deluxe

PREP TIME: 15 minutes
COOKING TIME: 10 minutes on stove top
SERVES: 6 to 8

12 ounces tri-color rotini pasta (or may substitute elbow macaroni)

1 each red, yellow, and orange bell peppers, sliced

1 cup black olives, pitted (buy them already pitted)

6½ ounces artichoke hearts, chopped (you may want to add more if you're an artichoke lover)

1 medium tomato, chopped

1 stalk celery, sliced

½ cup feta cheese

1 cup shredded pepper jack cheese

1 cucumber, unpeeled and thinly sliced

1 large bottle Italian dressing

Cook pasta per box directions; drain. Combine pasta and all other ingredients (except dressing) in large bowl; pour on dressing last and gently toss.

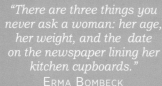

"There are three things you never ask a woman: her age, her weight, and the date on the newspaper lining her kitchen cupboards."
ERMA BOMBECK

Veggie Latkes

PREP TIME: 10 minutes
COOKING TIME: 15 minutes on stove top
SERVES: 4 to 6

＊A tasty and colorful variation of the traditional European and Jewish potato pancake; these little veggie pancakes with no added sugar will surely make your savory top.10 list.

1 medium zucchini, ends trimmed

1 large sweet potato, peeled

3 heaping tablespoons flour

1 teaspoon baking powder

¼ cup minced onion

1 large egg, slightly beaten

1 tablespoon minced garlic

¼ teaspoon salt

⅓ teaspoon pepper

4 to 6 tablespoons extra virgin olive oil

Slice zucchini lengthwise and remove seeds (if you miss some, no worries). Using food processor, grind zucchini and sweet potato to a fine consistency. Transfer to medium mixing bowl; add flour, baking powder, onion, egg, garlic, salt, and pepper. Mix into a thick batter.

Heat 2 tablespoons oil in large nonstick skillet over medium-high heat; spoon heaping tablespoons of batter onto skillet, flattening with the back of spoon to form 4 to 6 small pancakes (about 4 inches). Cook until edges are golden (2 to 3 minutes), then flip and cook until bottom is golden (about 3 minutes more). Adjust heat to prevent burning. Drain on paper towel. Repeat with remaining oil and rest of batter. Delicious served hot with applesauce on the side.

"Combat CCCB: Computer Chair Cauliflower Buns. Get that rear in gear."
DEBORA M. COTY, FROM
MORE BEAUTY, LESS BEAST

Martha's Yummy Potato–Garden Salad

PREP TIME: 20 minutes
COOKING TIME: 15 minutes on stove top, then refrigerate
SERVES: 6 to 8

6 eggs

3 pounds potatoes (or as many as you need)

1 cup shredded carrots

1 medium cucumber, sliced or diced

1 stalk celery, sliced

1 medium purple onion, chopped

1 to 2 cups mayonnaise (light okay)

2 tablespoons bacon bits

Black olives, pitted (optional)

Artichoke hearts, chopped (optional)

Salt and pepper to taste

1 tablespoon parsley and paprika (for garnish)

Boil eggs while simultaneously boiling potatoes in another pot (your choice whether to peel potatoes or not, but be sure to wash them regardless); once soft and cooled a bit, cut potatoes into bite-size cubes. Peel and cut up (slice or chop) boiled eggs; mix all ingredients together in large serving bowl and garnish with parsley and paprika. Refrigerate at least 1 hour before serving.

Chuckle Break:

Martha Bolton's Potato Salad Fiasco

Party guests and family have always raved about my homemade potato salad. But there *was* this one occasion. . .

My mother had specifically asked me to make my potato salad for the event. So I boiled the potatoes, added the other ingredients, and started mixing it all by hand. This is how those true chefs did it, I always told myself. You've got to "feel the food." "Be one with the veggies."

All was going well until I raised my hands out of the mix, and through all that ooey gooey goodness, I happened to notice that I only had nine of the ten acrylic fingernails that I had gone in with.

Now, I know some people bite their fingernails, but I didn't think anyone would want to bite into one, especially not in a potato salad! So I painstakingly went through the masterpiece chunk by chunk, shred by shred, hoping that I had lost the fingernail elsewhere and just hadn't noticed it. Maybe the salad could yet be saved.

But finally, there it was, at the bottom, hiding like a sunken treasure.

I ended up throwing the whole thing away and starting over from scratch. This time, though, I used spoons to mix it.

As usual, everyone raved about the potato salad. It really is a tasty recipe, with lots of healthy vegetables, and I was pleased that I had enough ingredients for that second batch.

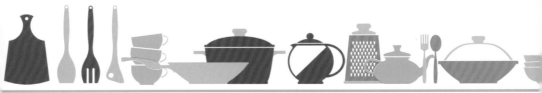

Carrot–Squash Sensation

PREP TIME: 15 minutes
COOKING TIME: 20 to 25 minutes in preheated 350° oven
SERVES: 6 to 8

4 to 6 yellow squash (2 cups when cooked)

2 carrots

2 tablespoons chopped onion

1 (10½ ounce) can cream of chicken soup

1 (4 ounce) jar diced pimientos

1 cup sour cream (light okay)

1 stick (8 tablespoons) butter, melted

1 (8 ounce) package seasoned herb stuffing

Wash and thinly slice squash; cook in covered microwavable dish with 1 tablespoon water for 5 minutes until soft; drain. Finely chop carrots in food processor. Combine veggies, onion, soup, pimientos, and sour cream. Add butter to package of stuffing; spread half on bottom of greased casserole dish. Place veggie mix on top of that and then finish with remaining half of stuffing atop veggies. Bake for 20 to 25 minutes; serve warm.

Shades of Green

Spinach–Broccoli Surprise

✳Happy memories of my sweet sister-in-law Suzi serving us this green-rich dish among the hundreds of green Florida Gator memorabilia that decorated her home.

PREP TIME: 15 minutes
COOKING TIME: 20 to 25 minutes in preheated 350° oven
SERVES: 6 to 8

2 (10 ounce) packages frozen chopped broccoli, thawed

2 (10 ounce) packages frozen chopped spinach, thawed

1 large sweet onion, diced

4 large eggs, beaten

1 cup mayonnaise (light okay)

2 (10½ ounce) cans cream of mushroom soup

2 cups shredded sharp cheddar cheese

1 teaspoon garlic powder

1 teaspoon salt

½ teaspoon pepper

8 to 10 Ritz crackers, crumbled

Drain thawed veggies and mix with other ingredients (except crackers) in greased 9x13-inch baking pan. Top with crumbled crackers; bake for 20 to 25 minutes.

"Popcorn for breakfast! Why not? It's a grain. Like grits, but with higher self-esteem."
JAMES PATTERSON

Zippity-do-da Coleslaw

PREP TIME: 10 minutes
COOKING TIME: none, refrigerate
SERVES: 6 to 8

1 head cabbage

1 large carrot

1 cup Marzetti Cole Slaw Dressing

1 tablespoon onion powder

1 tablespoon sour cream (light okay)

2 tablespoons pickle relish for a tangy twist (optional)

Chop cabbage and carrot in food processor to desired consistency; blend well with all other ingredients in medium mixing bowl. Chill at least 1 hour before serving.

"I demanded my butcher take the meat out from under the pink light and show me his prime rump in the daylight."
ERMA BOMBECK

Section 4

Company-Happy

ℓ ℓ ℓ ℓ ℓ

"After a good dinner one can forgive
anybody, even one's own relatives."
OSCAR WILDE

Think about my words,
as you would taste food.
JOB 34:3 CEV

Hors D'Oeuvres

Cha–Ching Chili Dip

PREP TIME: 5 minutes
COOKING TIME: 3 minutes in microwave
SERVES: 8 to 10

1 (15 ounce) can Hormel chili without beans

4 ounces cream cheese, softened

1 cup shredded 4-cheese Mexican blend

Fritos Scoops

Dump chili into medium microwavable baking dish (one that has a microwave-safe lid); add cream cheese. No need to stir yet. Cover and microwave on high for 2 minutes. Now stir until well blended. Top with cheese. If serving immediately, cover and zap in microwave for 1 minute until cheese melts. Serve with Fritos Scoops in festive bowl.

If not serving immediately, cover and refrigerate. When ready to serve, microwave (covered) for 2 to 3 minutes until cheese on top melts.

Tip: If you're entertaining on a smallish scale, substitute a 10½-ounce can Hormel chili (no beans), halve the other ingredients, and serve in a small dish.

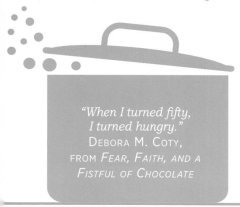
"When I turned fifty, I turned hungry."
DEBORA M. COTY,
FROM *FEAR, FAITH, AND A FISTFUL OF CHOCOLATE*

✻These dandy little savory munchies were my mother-in-law's signature welcome when we visited. I remember her fondly every time I serve them to smiling guests.

Oyster Cracker Eaties

PREP TIME: 5 minutes
COOKING TIME: none
SERVES: 6 to 8

1 package dry ranch dressing mix

½ cup oil

1 teaspoon dill weed

1 (12 ounce) box oyster crackers

Whisk together dry dressing mix, oil, and dill weed. Add crackers and stir until all liquid is absorbed. Serve in bowls or store in airtight containers for up to 1 week.

Tip: Buy a ranch dressing packet that says, "Add milk," but DON'T add milk; use it dry.

"My husband dislikes parties. He calls them the Varicose Olympics where people stand around all night talking about their dog's hysterectomies and eating bait off of little round crackers."
Erma Bombeck

Dilly Dip with Veggies

PREP TIME: 5 minutes
COOKING TIME: none
SERVES: 8 to 10

✳A wonderful starter to serve with cut-up fresh veggies.

1 cup mayonnaise (light okay)

1 cup sour cream (light okay)

1 tablespoon dry onion flakes

1 tablespoon dry parsley

1 teaspoon dill weed

1 teaspoon Worcestershire sauce

2 teaspoons Lowry's seasoning salt

Mix all ingredients thoroughly; serve with bite-size pieces of broccoli, cauliflower, celery, tomatoes, and carrots.

"'Tis an ill cook that cannot lick his own fingers."
WILLIAM SHAKESPEARE

Charleston Cheese Dip

PREP TIME: 10 minutes
COOKING TIME: 15 minutes in preheated 350° oven
SERVES: 8 to 10

1 cup mayonnaise (light okay)

16 ounces cream cheese, softened

2 cups shredded sharp cheddar cheese

4 green onions or 1 small red onion, chopped

12 Ritz crackers, crushed

2 ounces bacon bits

Mix mayonnaise, cream cheese, cheese, and onions. Spoon into greased 10-inch quiche dish (or pie plate). Top with crackers and bacon bits. (If made ahead of time, refrigerate in quiche dish and add crackers and bacon just before baking.) Bake for 15 minutes and serve warm with your fave dip cracker (I like Reduced Fat Wheat Thins).

Tip: If pinched for time, skip the oven and microwave on high for 3 minutes.

"Eating anything is socially acceptable before meals if you simply label it an hors d'oeuvre."
DEBORA M. COTY, INVENTOR OF SNICKERS AND CHEETOS HORS D'OEUVRES

Crabmeat Rapture

PREP TIME: 5 minutes
COOKING TIME: 2 minutes in microwave
SERVES: 6 to 8

✳I love this rich, appetizing dip I first tasted at a tennis tournament years ago; I always keep the ingredients on hand to whip it up on a moment's notice.

2 cups shredded sharp cheddar cheese

1 (6 ounce) can crabmeat

2 tablespoons mayonnaise (light okay)

1 tablespoon chopped onion flakes

Mix all ingredients together and heat on high for 2 minutes in small, covered microwavable serving bowl. Drain excess oil; serve hot with crackers.

"You can tell how long a couple has been married by whether they are on their first, second, or third bottle of Tabasco."
BRUCE BYE

Buffalo Chicken Cheese Dip

PREP TIME: 5 minutes
COOKING TIME: 3 minutes in microwave
SERVES: 8 to 10

8 ounces cream cheese, softened (light okay)

½ cup buttermilk ranch dressing

⅓ cup shredded mozzarella cheese

½ cup Tabasco sauce (if I'm not feeding my flame-loving son-in-law, I opt for Texas Pete extra mild buffalo wing sauce)

2 (5 ounce) cans Hormel chicken breast

Stir all ingredients together (add chicken last) until smooth. Microwave on high for 3 minutes and serve hot with crackers or chips.

Chuckle Break:

Turkey Memorial

You're gonna bust a gut over this hilarious Christmas cooking mishap from my friend, humorist and award-winning author, Martha Bolton. . .

I'll be the first to admit that I'm not the best cook in the world. You'll never see my recipes on the Food Network (although, Home Depot might be moved to display a few of them in their lumber aisle). My biggest problem is with my timing. I put the food on the stove or in the oven, and then I get distracted. A TV show catches my eye, I need to finish something on the computer, I go on vacation. . .

What happened one Christmas some years ago was not the result of any of that, though. It was an innocent mistake. My friend, Christian comedian Mark Lowry, had given my family a smoked turkey for Christmas. Now, I don't recall ever serving anything "smoked" before, other than maybe brownies (smoked, smoldering, what's the difference?). So I wasn't quite sure how to prepare this holiday bird. I had no idea that the term "smoked" meant that it had already been cooked.

Remembering that my mother always placed the turkey in the oven at night and then cooked it until the next day, I decided to do the same. I laid the bird in a pan, wrapped aluminum foil over it, and then baked it at 350 degrees until I served it the next day for the Christmas meal. It smelled delicious. That smoky aroma filled the entire house. My dinner guests, including a professional chef, were sure to be impressed.

But when I pulled back the aluminum foil, I was aghast to see that the

turkey was as black as coal, and the meat of its drumsticks had shrunk down, exposing several inches of bone. If you stood the poor thing up on its legs, it would've looked like a Cornish hen on stilts.

Mark almost cried, citing that it was the best-tasting turkey in the country and I had turned it into turkey jerky.

Luckily, I had also prepared a ham, which I had only baked a few hours, so the dinner wasn't a total disaster. But I learned something that day about the importance of timing, the futility of trying to impress others, and how God can turn our mishaps into opportunity.

God has His perfect timing. It was in His perfect timing that the first Christmas happened in Bethlehem over two thousand years ago. That babe, who left heaven to sleep on a bed of hay, didn't worry about impressing others, either. The One who humbly and obediently traded a throne for a manger of wood didn't think about what others would say about Him.

And God can turn even burnt turkey into opportunities: The opportunity to learn from my mishap—I now read the instructions on food gifts before incinerating them. I also know that watching someone's actions at a particular moment does not always give the whole story. Mom put the turkey in the oven at night, but what I didn't realize was that she got up in the middle of the night to take it out of the oven when it was done and then put it in the refrigerator. She was simply reheating it in the morning.

So look for God to show up at your Christmas gathering this year. He'll be there. In ways you might not even realize. Even in a burnt turkey.

*I could eat my weight in this yummy stuff; add a can of crabmeat occasionally for a little variety. It's palate pleasing, hearty, and a lot easier to make than it appears.

Cheese Broccoli Chowder

PREP TIME: 5 minutes
COOKING TIME: 15 minutes on stove top
SERVES: 6 to 8

1 medium onion, chopped

1 stick (8 tablespoons) butter, divided

1 (10 ounce) package frozen chopped broccoli

3 cups milk (low fat okay)

2 (10½ ounce) cans cream of chicken soup

3 cups shredded sharp cheddar cheese

In large soup pot, sauté onion with ½ stick butter until tender. At same time, place broccoli in microwavable bowl with 2 tablespoons water; cover and heat in microwave for 5 minutes until defrosted. Drain broccoli and add to soup pot with remainder of butter (it will melt faster if you cut it up and drop it in by small pieces), milk, soup, and cheese. Simmer over medium-low heat for 10 minutes, stirring frequently, until cheese completely melts.

"Worries go down better with soup."
JEWISH PROVERB

Pumpkin Soup

PREP TIME: 5 minutes
COOKING TIME: 15 minutes on stove top
SERVES: 6 to 8

2 (15 ounce) cans pumpkin

4 cups chicken broth (I use fat free)

½ cup brown sugar

1 teaspoon salt

½ teaspoon nutmeg

½ teaspoon cinnamon

1 cup half-and-half cream

Stir all ingredients (except half-and-half) together in large pot. Heat to near-boiling and then reduce to low. Add half-and-half and continue simmering for 10 minutes, stirring frequently. Serve in soup bowls with dash of cinnamon swirled on top.

*"Homemade meals—
especially mommy's
meals—are life's most
pleasant fuel."*
TERRI GUILLEMETS

Gorgeous Grape Salad

PREP TIME: 10 minutes
COOKING TIME: none, refrigerate
SERVES: 12 to 14

8 ounces sour cream (light okay)

8 ounces cream cheese, softened

8 tablespoons sugar

1 pound green grapes

1 pound red seedless grapes

½ pound brown sugar

12 ounces chopped pecans or walnuts

Blend together sour cream, cream cheese, and sugar. Fold in whole grapes and gently stir until well coated. Mix together brown sugar and nuts; sprinkle over grape mixture. Refrigerate until serving.

Tip: Recipe is easily halved for smaller groups.

Today's Menu:
A) Take it
B) Leave it

✳ My friend Betty gifted me with this super simple recipe thirty years ago. I've tweaked it a bit over the years and keep the ingredients on hand to make for all occasions.

Baked Corn Soufflé

PREP TIME: 5 minutes
COOKING TIME: 30 to 35 minutes in preheated 375° oven
SERVES: 6 to 8

2 (14¾ ounce) cans creamed corn

2 large eggs, beaten

3 tablespoons butter, melted

½ cup milk

3 tablespoons flour

1 tablespoon sugar

2 teaspoons seasoned salt

1 teaspoon garlic powder

1 (10 ounce) package frozen chopped broccoli (optional*)

Mix all ingredients together and pour into greased 9x13-inch baking dish. Bake for 30 to 35 minutes until soufflé no longer jiggles in the middle (be careful not to overbake into dryness).

Tip: You can use a 1½- or 2-quart casserole dish, but it will take a little longer to cook if the corn isn't spread out in a larger baking pan.

*If you opt to add broccoli, microwave frozen broccoli in covered microwavable dish with 1 tablespoon water for 5 minutes on high; drain.

"A good meal soothes the soul as it regenerates the body."
FREDERICK W. HACKWOOD

Sweet Potato Dumplings

PREP TIME: 15 minutes
COOKING TIME: 40 to 45 minutes in preheated
    350° oven
SERVES: 10 to 12

✳This crowd-pleaser could masquerade as dessert. My mother introduced me to these grand-slam yams, and whenever we serve them, people lunge for the last one.

1 (16 ounce) package frozen sweet potato patties, *don't* defrost (I use McKenzie's Yam Patties)

2 (8 count) cans refrigerated crescent rolls (I've used light and you couldn't tell)

1½ sticks (12 tablespoons) butter, melted

1 cup water

½ cup sugar

1 tablespoon cornstarch

1 teaspoon vanilla

Cinnamon to taste

Cut patties in half so you have 16 pieces; unroll and separate crescent roll dough into marked sections (triangles). Place potato piece at large end of triangle and roll patty up in dough, tucking in edges (like you're putting a little diaper on the sweet potato). Repeat for each patty. Place all 16 dumplings in greased 9x13-inch pan.

In small saucepan, combine butter, water, sugar, and cornstarch (mash out cornstarch lumps with spoon); stir over medium heat until sauce is slightly thickened (about 5 minutes). Remove from heat; stir in vanilla. Pour over dumplings and sprinkle lightly with cinnamon. Bake until lightly browned on top and no longer doughy on bottom (about 40 minutes).

Tip: Check the bottoms carefully for doneness; the first time I made these dumplings, I didn't let them cook long enough and they were still gooey on the bottom, although they looked done on top. Ugh. Before serving, spoon sauce from bottom of pan over dumplings so they glisten irresistibly.

"I promise to try harder to find fulfillment in carrot sticks rather than carrot cake. But by golly, wouldn't carrots taste much better dipped in cream cheese frosting?"
DEBORA M. COTY, FROM
MOM NEEDS CHOCOLATE

Squash Redemption

PREP TIME: 15 minutes
COOKING TIME: 15 to 20 minutes in preheated 350° oven
SERVES: 6 to 8

6 to 8 large yellow squash (2 cups when cooked; crookneck squash is best)

½ cup chopped onion

½ cup milk

2 large eggs, beaten

½ cup butter, melted

Salt and pepper to taste

10 to 12 Ritz crackers, crushed

1 cup shredded cheddar cheese

Wash and slice (no need to peel) squash; cook with onion until both are soft. (I use a pressure cooker so that it's done in about 8 minutes, but you may microwave or boil it—your preference.) Drain squash and onion; smash to mushy consistency with potato masher. (It's amazing how piles of squash cook down to such a tiny amount of squash paste!) Drain again. In same pot as squash (might as well not wash another mixing bowl, right?), add all other ingredients except crackers and cheese; mix well. Pour into greased casserole dish; top with crackers then cheese. Bake for 15 to 20 minutes until thoroughly heated and cheese melts.

> "I don't like food that's too carefully arranged; it makes me think that the chef is spending too much time arranging and not enough time cooking. If I wanted a picture I'd buy a painting."
> ANDY ROONEY

Sweet Onion Enchantment

PREP TIME: 10 minutes
COOKING TIME: 20 minutes in preheated 350° oven
SERVES: 4 to 6

4 large Vidalia (sweet) onions

1 cup milk (low fat okay)

1 cup chicken broth (fat free okay)

3 tablespoons flour

¼ cup slivered almonds

12 Ritz crackers, crumbled

½ cup shredded cheddar cheese

Chop onions coarsely in food processor; in covered microwavable dish, cook on high with 1 tablespoon water until tender (4 to 5 minutes). Drain and pour onions into greased 2-quart casserole dish. While microwaving onions, make sauce by mixing milk and chicken broth in saucepan over medium heat; slowly add flour, mashing out lumps with spoon. Cook until smooth and thick, stirring frequently. Add almonds to finished sauce before pouring over onions in baking dish; top with cracker crumbs then cheese. Bake until bubbly, about 20 minutes. (Casserole doesn't firm up completely but remains a bit saucy.)

"I only have a kitchen because it came with the house."
UNKNOWN

Chuckle Break:
Mystery Guest

I have to laugh about Martha Bolton's ill-fated Christmas turkey (pages 126–127) because I've undressed a few unfortunate birds myself, haven't you? That overcooked thigh meat just shrinks right up their naked little leg bones till it looks like the bird's wearing high-waters.

One day I was grousing about this very thing to my friend Ruth (who could give Rachel Ray a run for her money in a cook-off), and she suggested I spatchcock my next turkey.

"Um. . .*what?*" I asked, thoroughly confused. "Shuttlecock my bird? I don't have a badminton racket big enough to whack a sixteen-pound birdie. Will a tennis racket do?"

"No," she replied, trying to keep a straight face at my ignorance. "Spatchcock. It means remove the backbone and flatten out the turkey so it will cook evenly. The skin turns out crispy and the meat perfect. I won't serve turkey any other way."

I truly thought I was being bamboozled, but when I went online and searched "spatchcock," sure enough there was a video of an aproned man de-backboning a turkey then squashing it flat so the poor thing looked like it flew into the front grill of a semitruck.

So maybe I'll give it a try. And then I can tell everyone we're having a special guest for dinner this Thanksgiving—Alfred Spatchcock.

Entrées

Tantalizing Tamale Pie

✳I've cherished this little fiesta-in-a-pan ever since I got the recipe on a summer mission trip to Chicago when I was nineteen. Eat hearty!

PREP TIME: 15 minutes
COOKING TIME: 20 minutes in preheated 350° oven
SERVES: 8 to 10

1 (7 ounce) package corn bread mix

1 pound lean ground beef (or turkey)

1 large onion, chopped

1 (15 ounce) can black beans, drained

1 (15 ounce) can sloppy joe sauce

1 (17 ounce) can whole kernel corn

1 (6 ounce) can pitted olives, drained (optional)

1 teaspoon chili powder

⅛ teaspoon pepper

½ teaspoon garlic salt

2 cups shredded 4-cheese Mexican blend

Prepare corn bread batter per package directions; set aside. Brown meat and onions in 10-inch skillet; drain. Add all other ingredients (except cheese) plus ¼ cup water; mix well. Pour batter into greased 9x13-inch baking dish. Spoon meat mixture over batter to within ½ inch of edges, forming a border (which will be the edges of your crust). Top meat with cheese. Bake for 20 minutes or until cheese is bubbly and crust is light brown.

"There is no technique, there is just the way to do it. Now, are we going to measure or are we going to cook?"
FRANCES MAYES

Classy Ham Roll-Ups

PREP TIME: 15 minutes
COOKING TIME: 30 minutes in preheated 350° oven
SERVES: 4 to 6

1 (10½ ounce) can cream of chicken soup

½ cup milk (low fat okay)

1 (8 ounce) can refrigerated crescent rolls

1 cup shredded 4-cheese Mexican blend (or cheese of your choice)

½ cup cubed ham or 10 to 12 slices lunch meat ham cut into 2x1-inch strips (may substitute cooked chicken or turkey)

Bacon bits

Pour soup into small saucepan over medium heat; add milk, stirring occasionally until it reaches thick soup status (about 5 minutes). While soup is heating, unroll crescent roll dough; place 1 tablespoon cheese and generous amount of ham at wide end; roll up and place seam-side down in greased 9x13-inch baking pan. Drizzle soup over roll-ups in pan; sprinkle with remaining cheese then bacon bits. Bake for 30 minutes or until bubbly.

"You better cut the pizza in four pieces because I'm not hungry enough to eat six."
YOGI BERRA

Turkey–Frito Casserole

PREP TIME: 15 minutes
COOKING TIME: 20 minutes in preheated 350° oven
SERVES: 6 to 8

✳ While we're on a south-of-the-border roll, let me toss another zingy taste sensation your way. You'll love reincarnating Thanksgiving or Christmas turkey with a kick!

3 to 4 cups cooked turkey, chopped (I coarsely chop it in my food processor)

2 (10½ ounce) cans cream of chicken soup

2 cups cooked rice (white or brown, or a cup of each; I use instant)

3 to 4 dashes Worcestershire sauce, to taste

1 (4 ounce) can mushrooms or handful sliced fresh mushrooms (optional)

2 cups shredded cheddar cheese

2 cups Fritos, crunched

Combine all ingredients except cheese and Fritos in large mixing bowl; pour into greased 9x13-inch baking pan. Sprinkle with half the cheese; top with Fritos. Add remainder of cheese. Bake for 20 minutes. Serve with garlic bread and fruit.

"I think every woman should have a blowtorch."
JULIA CHILD

Homemade Chicken Nuggets

PREP TIME: 15 minutes
COOKING TIME: 10 minutes in preheated 325° oven + 10 minutes on stove top
SERVES: 4 to 6

2 large raw boneless, skinless chicken breasts

Salt and pepper to taste

2 cups pancake batter

1 large egg

½ cup olive oil (may need a little more)

½ cup barbeque sauce

Honey mustard to taste

Maple syrup to taste

Season chicken breasts with salt and pepper; cook in 325° oven for 10 minutes until chicken is about halfway done (still slightly raw). While chicken is cooling, make pancake batter per box directions, adding 1 egg. Cut breasts into bite-size pieces and place pieces from one breast into bowl of pancake batter, coating chicken well. In medium sauté pan over medium heat, pour enough oil to reach approximately halfway up sides of nuggets when placed in pan, 5 to 8 pieces at a time (don't crowd nuggets). Let one side fry for 2 minutes before flipping. Cook until golden brown. Repeat until all nuggets are done. Drain on paper towel and serve immediately with dipping sauce.

Dipping Sauce: Combine ½ cup barbeque sauce (I use Bubba Ray's Maple Brown Sugar BBQ Sauce) with 1 hefty squirt of honey mustard and 1 hefty squirt of maple syrup. Adjust quantities to taste.

"True love is the greatest thing in the world. . .except for a nice MLT: mutton, lettuce, and tomato sandwich, where the mutton is nice and lean [lip smack]; I love that."
BILLY CRYSTAL, AS MIRACLE MAX IN *THE PRINCESS BRIDE*

Skillet Pork Italiano

PREP TIME: 10 minutes
COOKING TIME: 20 minutes on stove top
SERVES: 4 to 6

1 pound pork tips (precut for stew)

2 tablespoons extra virgin olive oil

1 teaspoon minced garlic

2 zucchini, washed and thinly sliced

1 (14 ounce) can Italian-style chopped tomatoes

1 teaspoon sugar or Splenda

1 teaspoon Italian spice mix

1 teaspoon fennel

2 cups uncooked orzo (pasta shaped like rice)

In 12-inch skillet over medium-high heat, brown meat in olive oil, turning chunks frequently (don't worry about the inside being done at this point—you're only browning the outside). Add garlic and zucchini and reduce heat to medium; cook uncovered for another 2 minutes, still stirring to blend flavors. Add remaining ingredients (except orzo); cover and simmer over medium-low heat for 15 minutes, stirring occasionally. While meat is simmering, cook orzo per package directions. When orzo is done, drain and rinse; stir orzo into meat/veggie mixture and serve hot.

"You don't spring into good cooking naked. You have to have some training."
JULIA CHILD

Dear Aunt Suzi always made this excellent breakfast casserole when we came for weekend visits. It was such a joy to awaken to the marvelous aroma of this yummy casserole bubbling away in the oven. We thought that sometime during the night we must've taken a right turn into heaven.

Aunt Suzi's Breakfast Comfort

PREP TIME: 10 minutes (make day before and refrigerate overnight)
COOKING TIME: 30 minutes in preheated 350° oven
SERVES: 6 to 8

1 cup shredded cheddar cheese

6 eggs

2 cups milk (low fat okay)

1 teaspoon salt

¼ teaspoon dry mustard

6 slices bread, cut into ½-inch cubes

1 pound sausage, cooked and drained (I use turkey sausage)

Day ahead: Arrange bread, sausage, and cheese in greased 9x13-inch baking dish. Beat together eggs, milk, salt, and mustard, then pour over bread mixture. Cover and refrigerate overnight.

Remove from fridge 30 minutes before baking. Bake uncovered for 30 minutes until knife inserted near center comes out clean. Serve with croissants or biscuits and mixed fruit.

"Fast food is equivalent to pornography, nutritionally speaking."
STEVE ELBERT

Breakfast Quesadillas

PREP TIME: 15 minutes
COOKING TIME: 10 minutes on stove top
SERVES: 4 to 6

✳ *While we're on the subject of breakfast, I just have to share this yumdilicious finger food perfected by my should-a-been-a-chef son-in-law, Josh. Great for lunch and dinner, too.*

12 large eggs

½ medium onion, chopped (optional)

1 cup shredded mild cheddar cheese

1 cup cooked ground sausage or chopped ham

½ cup fresh or canned mushrooms (optional)

3 tablespoons extra virgin olive oil

8 large soft tortilla shells

Scramble eggs with onion (if desired); place in large mixing bowl. Add cheese, meat, and mushrooms (if desired); gently fold together. Spread thin layer of olive oil on one tortilla and place oil-side down on sauté pan over medium heat. Cover tortilla with egg/cheese/meat mixture; place second tortilla shell over mixture and spread thin layer of olive oil on top. Cook approximately 1 minute and then flip by placing a plate over top tortilla and turning pan over. Continue cooking until shells are golden brown and cheese glues tortillas together. Repeat for remainder of tortillas.

Tip: Cut each finished quesadilla in half or quarters for easier handling (this is where a good pair of food scissors comes in handy; if you don't have some, get some—you can't beat them for cutting pizzas, either!). For a little ha-cha-cha wake-up call, serve with sides of diced tomatoes (or salsa) and sour cream.

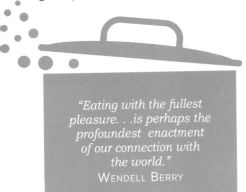

"Eating with the fullest pleasure. . .is perhaps the profoundest enactment of our connection with the world."
WENDELL BERRY

Chuckle Break:

Like a Little Syrup with Your Turkey?

"Julia Child once said, 'If the food is truly vile, then the cook must simply grit her teeth, bear it with a smile, and learn from her mistakes.' I remembered this sage advice just yesterday when I was attempting to make a white sauce at my daughter's house for chipped turkey on toast. I kept adding spoonfuls of flour from an unmarked crock, but the dadgum sauce simply would not thicken. I stirred and stirred and stirred. Finally growing suspicious that something was amuck, I dipped my finger in the flour and tasted it. It was confectioner's sugar."

DEBORA M. COTY

"A waffle is like a pancake with a syrup trap."
MITCH HEDBERG

Desserts

* The first time I tasted this outrageous treat, I thought I'd died and gone to the great ice cream parlor in the sky. This remarkable stuff takes banana splits to the next level.

Banana Split Pie

PREP TIME: 10 minutes
COOKING TIME: none, refrigerate
SERVES: 6 to 8

1 stick (8 tablespoons) butter

2 cups powdered sugar

2 large eggs

2 bananas, sliced

1 ready-made graham cracker crust

1 (8 ounce) can crushed pineapple, drained

4 ounces whipped topping

6 to 8 maraschino cherries

¼ cup chopped walnuts, peanuts, or pecans

Melt butter in microwave in covered medium mixing bowl; add powdered sugar and eggs. Beat with electric mixer until smooth. Spread bananas in bottom of piecrust. Pour filling mixture over bananas. Sprinkle pineapple evenly over filling. Cover with whipped topping and top with cherries and nuts. Refrigerate.

"The way to a girl's heart is through her Ghirardelli!"
DEBORA M. COTY,
FROM *MORE BEAUTY,
LESS BEAST*

Éclair Cake

✻This marvelous cake is actually more like a gigantic, irresistible chocolate éclair. It's ridiculously simple and has been one of my family's all-time favorites for decades.

PREP TIME: 15 minutes
COOKING TIME: none, refrigerate
SERVES: 8 to 10

2 (3½ ounce) packages French vanilla instant pudding mix

3 cups cold milk (for pudding)

8 ounces whipped topping

1 (14 ounce) box graham crackers

3 tablespoons butter

2 tablespoons white Karo syrup (light okay)

3 tablespoons milk (for frosting)

2 cups powdered sugar

4 tablespoons baking cocoa

With electric mixer, beat pudding mix with 3 cups milk until thickened; fold in whipped topping. Layer whole graham crackers (break to fit) in bottom of ungreased 9x13-inch pan. Cover with half of pudding. Add another layer of crackers, then remainder of pudding, then final layer of crackers.

To make frosting, melt butter in saucepan; remove from heat and add syrup, 3 tablespoons milk, powdered sugar, and cocoa. Mix until smooth. Pour over top graham cracker layer. Refrigerate.

Tip: In a time crunch, you may use canned chocolate fudge frosting (but I prefer the from-scratch kind).

"A party without cake is just a meeting."
JULIA CHILD

French Chocolate Cake

PREP TIME: 15 minutes
COOKING TIME: 13 to 15 minutes in preheated 425° oven
SERVES: 6 to 8

❋This fancy cake tastes just as delicious as it sounds. . .and yep, you read it right: only 15 minutes baking time! But be sure to make it at least an hour ahead so it can thoroughly cool before serving—the unique Paris café ambiance is created by the lovely toppings, which will melt if applied while the cake is still warm.

1 cup chocolate chips (I like to use ½ cup dark and ½ cup semisweet, but either is fine)

⅔ cup (11 tablespoons) butter

4 large eggs

¼ cup sugar

1 cup flour

1 teaspoon baking powder

⅓ cup chopped walnuts or pecans (optional)

1 (4 ounce) bar semisweet baking chocolate

1 can whipped cream

Melt chocolate chips in microwave for 2 minutes, stirring every 30 seconds (I melt chips in a glass measuring cup). Melt butter in separate covered microwavable mixing bowl; add melted chocolate to butter and stir. With electric mixer, beat eggs and sugar in small mixing bowl until light and airy (those French sure use a lot of bowls, don't they?); add chocolate/butter mixture and blend well.

Combine flour, baking powder, and nuts (if desired). Blend into batter using mixer on medium-low speed. Pour batter into greased 9-inch round glass pie plate or quiche dish and bake for 13 to 15 minutes until firm around edges (you want a 3-inch firm border). The cake should not become completely firm in the middle; the "unbaked" batter acts like a rich filling. Cool cake on counter for 10 minutes, then in fridge for expedited cooling if time is short.

"All you need is love. But a little chocolate now and then doesn't hurt."
CHARLES M. SCHULTZ

Just before serving, garnish cooled cake with grated or shaved (curls if you can manage them) semisweet baking chocolate (having not yet mastered curls, I use a carrot grater). Squirt fluffy whipped cream florets around top edge. (If you squirt the whipped cream on too early, it'll go flat before serving, so wait until the last minute.)

For years, my mama made this looks-way-harder-than-it-really-is treat, commonly referred to as, "That really good ice cream sandwich stuff." Recently, my writer pal Sharron shared the same recipe with me under the name Pit Stop Pie. Much catchier, don't you think? So here it is—you'll never find a quicker, easier, yummier dessert!

Pit Stop Pie

PREP TIME: 10 minutes
COOKING TIME: none, keep frozen
SERVES: 12 to 14

Chocolate syrup

Caramel ice cream topping

2 (12 count) boxes ice cream sandwiches

8 ounces whipped topping

½ cup chopped peanuts

Swirl chocolate syrup and caramel lightly on bottom of ungreased 9x13-inch pan; place layer of ice cream sandwiches on top of syrup and spread with whipped topping. Make second layer of sauces, ice cream sandwiches, and whipped topping. Drizzle chocolate syrup, caramel, and nuts on top; freeze until ready to serve.

Tip: 1 box ice cream sandwiches and 4 ounces whipped topping make a dandy 5x7-inch pan for a smaller audience (I use the same amount of nuts and sauces as for the large one).

"My derriere is a sacrifical altar to the Snickers god."
DEBORA M. COTY, FROM
MOM NEEDS CHOCOLATE

Chuckle Break:
I Won't Tell If You Won't
(Otherwise known as Deb's Confession)

The extra time I'd spent making the chocolate layer cake for our church's celebratory potluck was definitely worth it. The thing was simply gorgeous, slathered as it was in globs of rich chocolate icing like Lady Godiva might have fashioned herself.

I had to admire my culinary masterpiece as I carefully placed it on the floorboard of the car for the twenty-five-minute journey to church. I'd loaned my domed cake carrier to a friend, so I strategically placed items—the diaper bag, several umbrellas, my purse—around the base of the footed glass cake dish to stabilize the uncovered cake for the journey. I thought about covering it with cellophane wrap but was afraid the wrap would plaster to the newly applied frosting and ruin the Martha Stewart motif I'd worked so hard to achieve.

Nah, it'll be okay. We'll just take the corners nice and slow.

I bustled around to the other side of the car to buckle my baby in her infant seat and hollered to my four-year-old son to hurry or we'd be even later than we already were. Little Matthew sprinted to his car seat behind the driver. I asked if he needed me to help him get strapped in. "I do it all by my own self," was his reply, same as usual these days. So I made sure all our standard quarter-ton of church stuff was in the trunk while Spouse slid behind the wheel. Off we went.

Black Forest Pie

PREP TIME: 10 minutes
COOKING TIME: 30 minutes in preheated 350° oven
SERVES: 6 to 8

½ stick (4 tablespoons) butter

¾ cup sugar

⅓ cup baking cocoa

2 tablespoons flour

⅓ cup milk (low fat okay)

2 large eggs, lightly beaten

1 (21 ounce) can cherry or strawberry pie filling

1 unbaked pastry pie shell

Whipped cream (optional)

In saucepan, melt butter; stir in sugar, cocoa, flour, and milk until smooth. Bring to a boil over medium-high heat; stirring constantly, cook for 2 minutes until thickened. Remove from burner; add eggs and mix until blended. Stir in ⅓ of pie filling and pour into pastry shell. Bake for 30 minutes. Cool; top with remainder of pie filling. Just before serving, add whipped cream if desired.

"Seize the moment. Remember all those women on the Titanic *who waved off the dessert cart."*
ERMA BOMBECK

Menu Suggestions
and Grocery Lists

✱*Each of the following eight selections (A–H) contains 3 meal suggestions for one week (I figure with leftovers, crazy schedules, and eating out, 3 cooked dinners would be about right for most families) and the grocery items you'll need to pick up ahead of time (not including staples; see pages 14–15). You'll likely already have some of the ingredients, so don't panic at the length of the list; just electronically scan or photocopy the page, print a copy, and cross off the duplicates you've already accumulated. Like items are grouped together for stress-free shopping.*

Selection A

(recipes and ingredients for 3 meals)

DAY 1

"Nobody Makes It Better" Pizza (page 21)
Tossed Salad (create your fave)
Cookies & Cream Heaven (page 54)

DAY 2

Dilly Dip with Veggies (page 122)
Incredibly Easy Quiche (page 31)
To Die For Toffee (page 77)

DAY 3

Orzo-Veggie Chick-er-ole (page 27)
Squash Redemption (page 133)
Just Shoot Me Snickers Cake (page 150)

Grocery List

(menu ingredients for
all 3 meals in Selection A)

- [ ] shredded 4-cheese Mexican blend (1 cup)
- [ ] 1 (32 ounce) bag shredded cheddar cheese (save money and bother by buying this jumbo bag now; use what you need and freeze the rest for other recipes)
- [ ] shredded mozzarella cheese (8 ounces)
- [ ] sour cream (light okay)
- [ ] 1 (8 ounce) tub whipped topping (light okay)
- [ ] mayonnaise (light okay)
- [ ] 1 (2 count) box refrigerated piecrusts (I like Pillsbury)
- [ ] 1 package your choice cooked ham, turkey, or bacon
- [ ] cooked chicken (1 cup; either buy canned, rotisserie, or cook yourself)
- [ ] ready-made pizza crust (I like Mama Mary brand)
- [ ] pizza toppings of your choice (see recipe on page 21 for suggestions)
- [ ] 1 (10½ ounce) can condensed tomato soup
- [ ] 1 (10½ ounce) can cream of chicken soup

- [ ] 1 (14 ounce) package Oreos (reduced fat okay)
- [ ] 1 (14 ounce) box graham crackers
- [ ] 1 box German chocolate cake mix
- [ ] 3 (12 ounce) bags semisweet chocolate chips
- [ ] 2 (4 ounce) boxes Cookies 'n' Cream instant pudding mix
- [ ] powdered sugar
- [ ] orzo (pasta shaped like rice)
- [ ] Lowry's seasoning salt
- [ ] dill weed
- [ ] sea salt
- [ ] cocktail/party peanuts (1 cup; dry roasted okay)
- [ ] 1 (11 ounce) jar caramel sauce
- [ ] 1 small bag mini marshmallows
- [ ] your favorite tossed salad fixin's
- [ ] bite-size raw veggies (your choice: carrots, broccoli, cauliflower, celery, etc.)
- [ ] 6 to 8 large crookneck yellow squash
- [ ] 1 (12 ounce) steam-in-bag broccoli

Selection B

(recipes and ingredients for 3 meals)

DAY 1

Deb's Delicious Teriyaki Pork (page 36)
Summer Veggie Salad (page 116)
Magical Microwave Dessert (page 49)

DAY 2

Best Bean Soup Ever (page 94)
Martha's Yummy Potato-Garden Salad (page 109)
Pineapple Comfort Food (page 84)

DAY 3

Everybody's Fave Baked Spaghetti (page 25)
Fresh Brocco-flower Salad (page 114)
Black Forest Pie (page 153)

Grocery List

(menu ingredients for
all 3 meals in Selection B)

- ☐ 1 stick (8 tablespoons) real salted butter
- ☐ 1 dozen eggs
- ☐ sour cream (light okay)
- ☐ shredded cheddar cheese (3 cups)
- ☐ shredded sharp cheddar cheese (2 cups)
- ☐ grated Parmesan cheese (½ cup)
- ☐ whipped cream (optional)
- ☐ 1 refrigerated piecrust (comes in 2-count package)
- ☐ mayonnaise (light okay)
- ☐ 2 (10½ ounce) cans condensed tomato soup
- ☐ 1 (10½ ounce) can cream of mushroom soup
- ☐ fat-free chicken broth (2 cups)
- ☐ 1 (4 ounce) can mushrooms (or may opt for fresh)
- ☐ 1 (15 ounce) can diced tomatoes (optional)

- [ ] black olives, pitted (optional)
- [ ] artichoke hearts (optional)
- [ ] 1 (15 ounce) can each: pinto beans, dark red kidney beans, fat-free refried beans
- [ ] 1 (16 ounce) box angel hair pasta
- [ ] teriyaki sauce (½ to ¾ cup)
- [ ] ketchup
- [ ] 2 (20 ounce) cans pineapple tidbits in unsweetened juice
- [ ] 3 (21 ounce) cans strawberry or cherry pie filling (2 need to be the same)
- [ ] 1 cake mix (your favorite flavor)
- [ ] 1 can mandarin oranges (½ cup)
- [ ] golden raisins (½ cup)
- [ ] sunflower nuggets or kernels (⅓ cup)
- [ ] 1 pork roast, any size (I prefer 3- to 4-pound Boston butt)
- [ ] ground beef or turkey (1 pound)
- [ ] potatoes (3 pounds)
- [ ] 6 green onions

- [ ] 2 onions (1 large, 1 small)
- [ ] 2 purple onions
- [ ] celery
- [ ] 2 medium cucumbers
- [ ] 2 carrots
- [ ] 1 bunch broccoli or cauliflower (see recipe on page 114)
- [ ] 1 (10 ounce) package frozen peas

Selection C

(recipes and ingredients for 3 meals)

DAY 1

Workday Salvation (page 29)
Garlic Rolls (purchase your fave)
Luscious Lime Pie (page 53)

DAY 2

Cha-Ching Chili Dip (page 120)
Delicious Fish Fillets (page 93)
Carrot-Squash Sensation (page 111)
Peaches & Cream Pie (page 85)

DAY 3

Cheese Broccoli Chowder (page 128)
California Cuisine (page 105)
Apple Fries (page 88)

Grocery List

(menu ingredients for
all 3 meals in Selection C)

☐ sour cream (24 ounces; light okay)

☐ cream cheese (4 ounces)

☐ cheddar cheese spread (2 cups)

☐ shredded 4-cheese Mexican blend (1 cup)

☐ shredded sharp cheddar cheese (3 cups)

☐ 1 (2 count) package refrigerated piecrusts

☐ 1 (13½ ounce) tub whipped topping (light okay)

☐ your favorite brand garlic rolls or bread (ready-made saves time)

☐ 1 (15 ounce) can Hormel chili without beans

☐ red wine vinegar

☐ 1 (13 ounce) can sliced peaches

☐ golden raisins (½ cup)

☐ 1 (15 ounce) can black-eyed peas

☐ 1 (11 ounce) can shoepeg corn

- [ ] 3 (10½ ounce) cans cream of chicken soup
- [ ] 1 (8 ounce) package seasoned herb stuffing
- [ ] 1 (4 ounce) jar diced pimientos
- [ ] 1 bag Fritos Scoops
- [ ] McCormick Grill Mates Roasted Garlic & Herb seasoning
- [ ] almond flavoring
- [ ] 3 ready-made graham cracker crusts
- [ ] 1 (14 ounce) can sweetened condensed milk
- [ ] 1 (21 ounce) can apple pie filling
- [ ] 1 fresh lime or other garnish for Luscious Lime Pie (see page 53)
- [ ] lemon juice
- [ ] plum tomatoes (1 cup chopped)
- [ ] fresh parsley + green onions (½ cup each)
- [ ] 2 medium onion
- [ ] 2 carrots
- [ ] 2 avocados
- [ ] 4 to 6 yellow crookneck squash

- [ ] caramel fruit dip
- [ ] ground beef or turkey (1 pound)
- [ ] 4 fresh or frozen fish fillets (your choice: I like tilapia)
- [ ] 1 (10 ounce) package frozen chopped spinach
- [ ] 1 (10 ounce) package frozen chopped broccoli
- [ ] 1 (12 ounce) can frozen limeade

Selection D

(recipes and ingredients for 3 meals)

DAY 1

Skillet Pork Italiano (page 140)
Sweet Potato Dumplings (page 132)
Triple Chocolate Threat (page 83)

DAY 2

Beef 'n' Bean Bonanza (page 24)
Zippity-do-da Coleslaw (page 117)
Banana Pudding (page 87)

DAY 3

Cures Anything Chicken-Veggie Soup (page 96)
Harvest Bread (page 71)
Guess Again Cookie Bars (page 78)

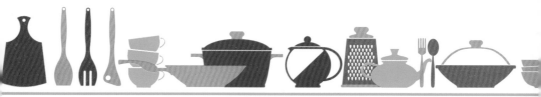

Grocery List

(menu ingredients for
all 3 meals in Selection D)

- [ ] 1 (16 ounce) roll chocolate chip cookie dough
- [ ] sour cream (light okay)
- [ ] 2 (8 count) cans refrigerated crescent rolls (light okay)
- [ ] 1 (15 ounce) can each: mixed vegetables, whole kernel corn, garbanzo beans
- [ ] 1 (4 ounce) can mushrooms (optional)
- [ ] 1 (8½ ounce) can sweet green peas or lima beans
- [ ] 2 (15 ounce) cans pork and beans
- [ ] 1 (10½ ounce) can condensed tomato soup
- [ ] 1 (14 ounce) can Italian-style chopped tomatoes
- [ ] 1 (8 ounce) can pumpkin
- [ ] 1 (3 ounce) package Ramen noodles, chicken flavor
- [ ] 1 box rolled oats (quick oats okay)
- [ ] raisins (¼ cup)
- [ ] chopped pecans or walnuts (optional)

- ☐ mini marshmallows (optional)
- ☐ 1 (12 ounce) box vanilla wafers
- ☐ Oreos (reduced fat okay)
- ☐ 1 (7½ ounce) package Martha White Chocolate-Chocolate Chip muffin mix
- ☐ your favorite ingredient options for Guess Again Cookie Bars (see page 78)
- ☐ chicken broth (4 cups; fat free okay)
- ☐ chicken bouillon cubes
- ☐ orzo (pasta shaped like rice)
- ☐ fennel
- ☐ pickle relish (optional)
- ☐ 1 bottle Marzetti Cole Slaw Dressing
- ☐ ground beef (1 pound)
- ☐ pork tips (1 pound; precut for stew)
- ☐ cooked chicken (2 cups; either buy canned, rotisserie, or cook yourself)
- ☐ 1 (16 ounce) package frozen sweet potato patties (I like McKenzie's Yam Patties)
- ☐ 1 head cabbage

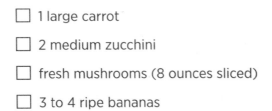

☐ 1 large carrot

☐ 2 medium zucchini

☐ fresh mushrooms (8 ounces sliced)

☐ 3 to 4 ripe bananas

Selection E

(recipes and ingredients for 3 meals)

DAY 1

Honey Mustard Chicken & Veggies (page 38)
Gorgeous Grape Salad (page 130)
Éclair Cake (page 145)

DAY 2

Greek-Style Orzo Chicken Salad (page 92)
Fresh Green Bean Parmesan (page 115)
Banana Split Pie (page 144)

DAY 3

Charleston Cheese Dip (page 123)
Quick as a Wink Stir-Fry (page 22)
Pit Stop Pie (page 147)

Grocery List

(menu ingredients for
all 3 meals in Selection E)

- [ ] cream cheese (24 ounces, light okay)
- [ ] sour cream (8 ounces, light okay)
- [ ] shredded sharp cheddar cheese (2 cups)
- [ ] shredded mozzarella cheese (1 cup)
- [ ] feta cheese (4 ounces)
- [ ] 2 (12 count) boxes ice cream sandwiches
- [ ] 2 (8 ounce) tubs whipped topping (light okay)
- [ ] grated Parmesan cheese (½ cup)
- [ ] mayonnaise (light okay)
- [ ] deli-style mustard
- [ ] black olives, pitted
- [ ] honey or maple syrup
- [ ] honey mustard or Dijon mustard
- [ ] 1 jar maraschino cherries
- [ ] 1 (8 ounce) can crushed pineapple

- [ ] 2 (3½ ounce) packages French vanilla instant pudding mix
- [ ] white Karo syrup (light okay)
- [ ] powdered sugar (4 cups)
- [ ] 1 (14 ounce) box graham crackers
- [ ] 1 each chocolate and caramel ice cream sauce
- [ ] orzo (pasta shaped like rice; 8 ounces)
- [ ] 1 ready-made graham cracker crust
- [ ] red wine vinegar
- [ ] bacon bits (2 ounces)
- [ ] cashews (optional)
- [ ] cocktail/party peanuts
- [ ] walnuts or pecans (14 ounces)
- [ ] raw boneless, skinless chicken breasts (3 to 4 pounds; for different recipes)
- [ ] lemon juice
- [ ] 8 green onions/scallions
- [ ] 1 cucumber (optional)
- [ ] 1 red bell pepper (optional)
- [ ] cherry tomatoes or 1 medium tomato

- [ ] 3 large potatoes
- [ ] 3 carrots
- [ ] 2 bananas
- [ ] green and red seedless grapes (1 pound each)
- [ ] sliced fresh mushrooms (6 to 8 ounces)
- [ ] fresh green beans (1 pound)
- [ ] 1 (12 ounce) bag frozen stir-fry vegetables

Selection F

(recipes and ingredients for 3 meals)

DAY 1

Crispy Cheddar Chicken (page 34)
Grandma's Copper Pennies (page 60)
Sweet Onion Enchantment (page 134)

DAY 2

Classy Ham Roll-Ups (page 137)
Pumpkin Soup (page 129)
Kicky Quicky Pasta Salad (page 33)
Mudbar Ecstasy (page 89)

DAY 3

Crabmeat Rapture (page 124)
Fabulous 15-Minute Fettuccine (page 35)
Hearty 4-Bean Salad (page 103)
Ooooey Gooey Brownies (page 80)

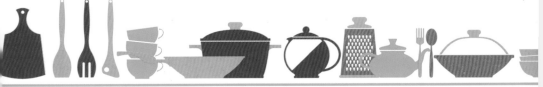

Grocery List

(menu ingredients for
all 3 meals in Selection F)

- [ ] half-and-half (1 cup)
- [ ] 1 (8 ounce) can refrigerated crescent rolls
- [ ] 4-cheese shredded Mexican blend (1 cup)
- [ ] sour cream (12 ounces, light okay)
- [ ] feta cheese (8 ounces)
- [ ] shredded pepper jack cheese (8 ounces)
- [ ] shredded sharp cheddar cheese (2 cups)
- [ ] grated Parmesan cheese (½ cup)
- [ ] cubed ham or lunch meat (turkey or chicken okay)
- [ ] pepperoni (about 3 ounces)
- [ ] 2 (15 ounce) cans pumpkin
- [ ] 2 (10½ ounce) cans cream of chicken soup
- [ ] 1 (10½ ounce) can condensed tomato soup
- [ ] 1 (15 ounce) can black olives, pitted

- [ ] 1 (4 ounce) can sliced mushrooms
- [ ] 2 (15 ounce) cans each garbanzo beans (chickpeas) and black beans
- [ ] 1 (15 ounce) can each light and dark kidney beans
- [ ] 1 (6 ounce) can crabmeat
- [ ] chicken broth (you'll need 5 cups total for several different recipes)
- [ ] 2 bottles of your favorite Italian dressing (for 2 different recipes)
- [ ] 1 (8 ounce) box fettuccine noodles
- [ ] 1 (12 ounce) box rotini pasta
- [ ] baking cocoa (½ cup)
- [ ] dry mustard
- [ ] self-rising flour
- [ ] powdered sugar
- [ ] shortening (1 cup)
- [ ] walnuts or pecans (optional)
- [ ] 1 (12 ounce) bag semisweet chocolate chips
- [ ] slivered almonds (¼ cup)

- ☐ Ritz crackers
- ☐ artichoke hearts (3 ounces)
- ☐ 4 large (Vidalia) sweet onions
- ☐ 1 each red, yellow, and orange bell peppers
- ☐ 2 bell peppers
- ☐ 2 stalks celery
- ☐ 3 medium onions
- ☐ carrots (2½ pounds)
- ☐ 4 raw boneless, skinless chicken breasts
- ☐ shrimp (1 pound, fresh or frozen)

Selection G

(recipes and ingredients for 3 meals)

DAY 1

Hot Chicken Salad (page 61)
Parmesan Nuggets (page 68)
Strawberry Pizza (page 74)

DAY 2

Humdinger Chili (page 43)
No Yeast Whole Wheat Bread (page 99)
Blueberry Delight (page 90)

DAY 3

Starke Raving Chicken (page 30)
Veggie Latkes (page 108)
French Chocolate Cake (page 146)

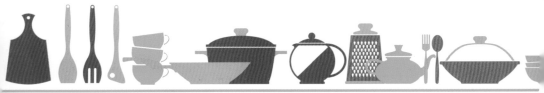

Grocery List

(menu ingredients for
all 3 meals in Selection G)

- ☐ cream cheese (6 ounces)
- ☐ sour cream
- ☐ shredded swiss cheese (8 ounces)
- ☐ whipped topping (16 ounces; light okay)
- ☐ 1 can whipped cream
- ☐ grated Parmesan cheese (6 ounces)
- ☐ grated cheddar cheese
- ☐ 1 (10 ounce) can refrigerated biscuits (butter flavor)
- ☐ butter (4 sticks)
- ☐ 1 dozen eggs
- ☐ mayonnaise (light okay)
- ☐ chicken broth (½ cup)
- ☐ 1 (15 ounce) can Ranch Style beans
- ☐ 1 (15 ounce) can Kidney beans (light or dark red)
- ☐ 1 package chili seasoning

- [ ] 2 (10½ ounce) cans tomato soup
- [ ] 3 (10½ ounce) cans cream of chicken soup
- [ ] 1 (14½ ounce) can diced tomatoes
- [ ] 1 (14 ounce) box graham crackers
- [ ] 1 (21 ounce) can blueberry pie filling
- [ ] 1 large box vanilla instant pudding mix
- [ ] 1 bag semisweet or dark chocolate chips
- [ ] 1 (4 ounce) bar semisweet baking chocolate
- [ ] honey
- [ ] raw chicken strips (1 pound)
- [ ] ground beef or turkey (2 pounds)
- [ ] cooked chicken (2 cups; can either buy canned, rotisserie, or cook yourself)
- [ ] 1 (8 ounce) jar strawberry glaze
- [ ] celery (2 cups chopped)
- [ ] lemon juice
- [ ] 1 large white potato
- [ ] 1 large sweet potato
- [ ] 1 medium zucchini

- [ ] 2 onions
- [ ] 1 green bell pepper (optional)
- [ ] 6 to 8 Honey Gold potatoes or new (small) potatoes
- [ ] fresh strawberries (1 quart)
- [ ] Stove Top stuffing
- [ ] slivered almonds (1 cup)
- [ ] walnuts or pecans (optional)
- [ ] powdered sugar
- [ ] whole wheat flour (2 cups)

Selection H

(recipes and ingredients for 3 meals)

DAY 1

Homemade Chicken Nuggets (page 139)
Sweet Potato Home Fries (page 106)
Incredibly Easy Cheesecake (page 48)

DAY 2

Mexican Salad (page 32)
Banana-Berry Loaf (page 67)

DAY 3

Mimi's Blue Ribbon Chicken Gumbo (page 63)
Pasta Salad Deluxe (page 107)
Chocolate Brickle (page 76)

Grocery List

(menu ingredients for
all 3 meals in Selection H)

- [ ] shredded 4-cheese Mexican blend (2 cups)
- [ ] sour cream (8 ounces)
- [ ] 1 stick (8 tablespoons) real salted butter
- [ ] cream cheese (16 ounces)
- [ ] feta cheese (½ cup)
- [ ] whipped topping (12 ounces; light okay)
- [ ] shredded pepper jack cheese (1 cup)
- [ ] mayonnaise (light okay)
- [ ] 2 (15 ounce) cans Hormel chili without beans
- [ ] 1 large bottle Italian dressing
- [ ] 1 (21 ounce) can strawberry or cherry pie filling
- [ ] 1 (10½ ounce) can cream of chicken soup
- [ ] 1 (5 ounce) can sliced water chestnuts
- [ ] 1 (12 ounce) box tri-color rotini pasta

- [ ] artichoke hearts (6½ ounces)
- [ ] black olives, pitted (1 cup)
- [ ] maple syrup
- [ ] honey mustard
- [ ] barbeque sauce (½ cup; recommend Bubba Ray's Maple Brown Sugar)
- [ ] pancake batter
- [ ] 1 (9 ounce) bag Fritos
- [ ] potato chips
- [ ] 2 ready-made graham cracker crusts
- [ ] milk or dark chocolate melting wafers (12 ounces) or semisweet chocolate chips (12 ounces)
- [ ] strawberry jam (1 cup)
- [ ] lemon juice
- [ ] saltine crackers
- [ ] chopped walnuts or pecans (1¼ cups)
- [ ] 2 large raw boneless, skinless chicken breasts
- [ ] cooked chicken (1 cup; either buy canned, rotisserie, or cook yourself)
- [ ] 1 head lettuce

- [ ] 2 stalks celery
- [ ] 2 tomatoes
- [ ] 1 cucumber
- [ ] 1 each red, yellow, and orange bell peppers
- [ ] 4 sweet potatoes
- [ ] 4 to 5 ripe bananas

Recipe Index

T

V

W

Z

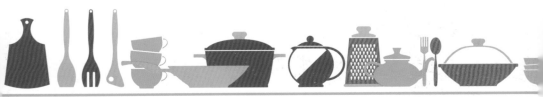